CREATING YOUR OWN REAL ESTATE CASH MACHINE

CREATING YOUR OWN REAL ESTATE CASH MACHINE

Discover the Secrets To How I Created Millions Of Dollars In Equity And Cash Flow 2nd Edition

A Real Estate Lifestyle
and Philosophy
for Financial Freedom

2nd Edition

Alan Schnur

ISBN-13: 9781537606132
ISBN-10: 1537606131

Contact the Author

Alan Schnur

Email: alan@alanschnur.com
http://www.alanschnur.com/

CONTENTS

Robert Frost's famous poem "The Road Not Taken" beautifully illustrates the dilemma of choices. Frost tells us that we like to think we are contrarians, but in fact, at the moment of judgment, it's impossible to tell where each choice will lead us, and we can never go back.

INTRODUCTION

What an adventure! In the five years since the first edition, real estate markets have changed dramatically, and I greatly enjoyed updating this text. When I completed my first version, real estate as an investment was unpopular and depressed. In less than five years since, values have come roaring back. In the downturn, I bought over 2,000 units and have sold most of them to reposition my assets. I also bought hundreds of single family homes.

I invite you to sit back and relax as we catch up and figure out where we are headed this time! I think 2017 will be an interesting year for commercial real estate markets. I don't want you to be afraid, but rather, well aware and prepared. Currently, we are in a strong up cycle and lending is still easy to come across for most of us. If you own property that you have thought about selling, now would be a good time. We are in good times! If you're currently looking at a new property, though, I advise more caution. It's better to lock up long-term debt with a healthy interest rate.

If you have not been on this journey for the past five years, introductions are in order. I consider myself a traveling real estate entrepreneur.

Being able to find a Starbucks just about anywhere in the world has given me this opportunity to turn my ideas into an investing strategy system that I'm excited to put down on paper and share with you. It's not been 20 years since I started this journey, and I have seen a lot.

One of my favorite parts of this journey is traveling around the world. From the Taj Mahal to 19,341 feet at the top of Mount Kilimanjaro; from hiking some of most scenic trails in Northern Thailand and expeditions through the Golden Triangle where Thailand, Burma, and Laos converge, arise some of my most awe inspiring adventures that shape and propel my philosophy and lifestyle.

My travel experiences range from enlightening adventures at a benchmark Elephant Camp in Southeast Asia for elephant welfare and conservation and learning a great deal through my adventures camel trekking through the Australian Outback and Central Flinders Ranges; to diving the outer edge of the Great Barrier Reef. My explorations through my travel adventures are truly amazing and I am fortunate to have the financial freedom to travel the world because of my business lifestyle.

It's human nature to want to buy low and sell high, and with that psychology comes market cycles that we will to explore a bit.

For one thing, most of us assume we should buy real estate only in our own back yards.

With two decades of experience in the stock market and commodities markets, I'm living proof that it is possible to buy and manage anywhere in the world and profit from the ups and downs of local economies. In this day and age, we no longer need to be locked into our immediate vicinity. We are fortunate to live in a country that, despite some problems, still seems to be the world's top choice for buying a piece to call home. Because of this, I think apartments are super-powerful profit machines that can make us very rich and grateful to have 3,500 miles coast to coast to pick from.

I have found a path of progress. We recently purchased a 125-unit complex in the middle of a suburban city. Six months later, we watched multiple housing developments start up and major retailers move into the area, including Starbucks and McDonald's. How did we know? Was it luck? Not really. We simply were able to track a huge spike in housing permits and new employment—a great indicator of what's to come.

New employment is powerful, too. Think about all the jobs it takes to support everyone from high-paid executives to minimum wage workers. They all need supermarkets, medical care and gas stations. Employment is contagious, so now we own a Class C complex that we easily could reposition into a Class B, and it is surrounded by new Class A structures. The path of progress is golden—a formula for instant wealth. My students and friends have made fortunes through buying at this time. I know you can, too!

In a flipper's market, the path becomes a little tricky, but now's still not a good time to be cheap if you know you have a good deal. You're already getting a discount and the market is moving fast. Remember: it only take a slight change to the asset or good timing before you're able to mark up the complex a few thousand dollars per door. It's easy money—try not to pass it up! The standard refrain is "Location, location, location," and while this is nice, if there is money to be made, sell and move on to the next!

The process for making millions of dollars is quite simple. You need to find an area that is beaten up and buy as many properties as possible. If you have done your homework and the economics are about to turn, then BUY! You will find in market upswings and in improving areas that the permitting and new construction phase takes months, if not years, to begin. But this simple supply and demand issue creates a better situation for you.

The same holds true for the opposite, of course. If employers are fleeing and the area is declining, then SELL! The challenge of maintaining current market standards is only going to get worse. This could be the beginning of a downward spiral for the property. You might have to lower rents to keep tenants. In any event, you might want to take a good, hard look at the situation and review your exit strategy.

The trick is buying below market replacement cost. When I first started out, I planned to build houses and retire using earnings off the cash flow, but that didn't last long! I learned quickly that I was able to purchase government distressed properties at half the price it would cost to build.

The same holds true for multifamily apartment buildings. There simply is not enough land, and if it costs twice as much to build, why not just keep the complex the way it is? It's like buying a dollar for 50 cents. I recently watched an out-of-town buyer pay a record price for a property that was 30 years old. Turns out, he was right! That area of town is hot and values are going through the roof. His exact words to me were, "Alan, it would cost double to build, so I bought it."

What goes up must come down!

My formula for flipping your way up the food chain:

1. Find a market that has been devastated.
2. Sell my assets in a stellar area at the peak of the market.
3. Move my profits to the devastated market and a higher class.
4. Buy as much property as I can.
5. Cash out of a hot market and buy into a new market and higher class.
6. Turn up my money-raising efforts now that I have entered and exited a market with success.
7. Rinse and repeat!

I also have used this method to swap assets. **My formula for swapping assets, TAX FREE:**

1. Buy eight houses.
2. Sell.
3. Buy a small apartment building with the profits.
4. Sell the small apartment building.
5. Buyer a bigger apartment building.
6. Sell the bigger apartment building.
7. Buy a housing community from a builder.
8. Buy an assisted living apartment deal.
9. Develop.

Get the picture?

You must learn how to attract the best real estate deals. A lot of this will come through your networking abilities. I can't stress how important it is to always stay in touch with your team and take care of them! Buy them lunch; attend an event with them. You must take care of them so that you can fill your time to its highest and best use. Finding a profitable deal will help attract the money. Soon, you will be just the one in the middle.

Another way to find the right deal, or the right people, is to attend one of my events. As the saying goes, like-minded people attract each other. I met my business partner, Dave, at an apartment seminar, and we have gone on to conduct more than 15 deals with each other.

The Wealth-Building Secret of Apartment Buildings

Move to bigger deals as soon as you can! It takes the same amount of effort to do a $100,000 deal as a million-dollar deal. Another reason is that larger properties throw off more cash flow, so you can hire more qualified workers to run it for you.

The knowledge my friends and students acquired from my programs lessened their hurdles and reduced their fears—not to mention putting time on their side. My time-saving techniques can create wealth that saves you years of work.

It doesn't take much to get started. In fact, you should keep your regular job. When I first began, I didn't spend more than three hours a week—only about half an hour per day—building my systems and making contacts. I greatly looked forward to that half hour a day and the escape it provided. It felt good to plan and implement an exit strategy from my current job. I realized that if the price of a piece of real estate was too high, then maybe I could pay for it as long as the seller would accept my terms.

My formula to put you on the path to progress:

1. Buy a Class C property in a Class A area.
2. Convert it to a Class B property.
3. Watch retail stores move in.
4. Move rents as property quickly appreciates.
5. Successfully exit.

I hope you can see that the path of progress is not just about land and property. It's also about people: the type of tenant you attract. I learned that there is "cash in trash" but it's not as easy to collect as it is from tenants with checking accounts, valid credit cards and high-paying, steady jobs.

Great deals find great people, but great deals won't last long if you can't do something great with them. Always be building your war chest of cash and connections so that you can move fast and close deals as they arise.

Get in the game and transact your first deal. It's okay if it's small, as long as you take action. The process of closing is addicting! If you're like me, after you do it one time, you will want to do it again and again, and before long, the cash flow from your deals will exceed the pay from your job. At that point, you will need to decide if you want to quit and go full time into real estate, or just work less—what I call a high-quality problem!

You don't pay for your property management company—your tenants do, as long as you use the systems and the negotiation tactics I share with my students at my events.

The key to success in investing in apartment complexes is the property management company.

My three ways to rocket wealth to the moon:

1. Value play—find problems and fix them.
2. Refinance your property, tax-free.
3. Sell your property with a 1031 exchange, then refinance.

Deferred gratification is a term we hear all the time, especially when we listen to some of the so-called, great financial "real estate gurus" talk about investing. Their mantras are "Buy and hold," "Slow and steady wins the race," or "It's not timing the market, but time in the market."

These can be great in theory—that is, if you like to wait! When it comes to making money—especially in terms of building your net worth and cash flow, and achieving your financial dreams—most people trade their time for money. And that's a bad trade!

In fact, time can be the worst enemy for those who want to be better off financially. Most people do not understand the value of their time and how it can be used to create a massive amount of wealth. If you are following the conventional wisdom, do you know when you will get the chance to say, "I'm rich?" Unfortunately, most people will never get that chance.

While there are very few legitimate, "get rich quick" methods (legal ones, anyway), it is equally senseless to get rich slowly! After all, any of us could toil away for 20, 40 or 60 or more years, only to have our wealth snatched away from us through any of a number of unforeseeable circumstances. The future is uncertain, which is why it helps to not only know how to acquire wealth within a relatively short time, but also how to keep (or reacquire) wealth as needed.

I want to introduce to you to a process that will teach you how to reinvest some of your profits in what already is proven to work. I call this process my "Massive Apartment Complex System." I will teach you to scale up and buy bigger apartment buildings, while also reaping the bigger cash flows that comes with them. I also will share my revolutionary ideas and tactics that give you the advantage in our too-often uncertain economy.

It's an honor and privilege to reintroduce the simple, old idea of cash flow. This concept changed my life, and it could do the same for you! The problem today is that most investors focus on instant gratification or "chunks of cash." For the investor, this turns out to be just another J.O.B., because the sale of one asset leads to the purchase of another—a vicious cycle. Why sell the goose that lays golden eggs, or kill the cows that give you milk every day? I have been teaching people for decades how they can cash flow their dreams. Together, we will look at my system and discover how I amassed millions of dollars of real estate!

How This Book Will Help You

This book will help you understand why today's real estate market is the "perfect storm" for acquiring houses, apartment buildings and retail strips as profitable investments. Remember: Just because you acquire these properties does not mean you need to hold them for years, learn to fix toilets or even collect rental checks from tenants. No! Those are old ideas that can be easily outsourced. What it does mean is that you will have to learn strategies, systems and resources for making better choices about cash flowing apartment buildings.

Once you complete this book, you will have a thorough understanding of:

- Why apartment buildings make perfect sense as an investment, whether you are a new or experienced investor.
- How you can increase your profits exponentially in real estate when dealing with apartments.

- How to properly evaluate a property before making an offer, so you know whether to proceed or move on.
- Where to find the cash to make these investments—some financing sources may surprise you!
- How to structure your purchase offer so it makes the most sense for your specific real estate investing goals.
- How to position your property to either flip or hold—and how to make the most profit from either decision.
- How to continue the wealth-building process for years to come!

NOW is the time to take advantage of all the positives of investing in apartment buildings. Why wait? Slow and steady doesn't always win the race, but knowing how to invest for profit right now certainly does! Discover how you can cash flow your dreams and speed up the wealth process.

Let's get started!

About Alan

Alan Schnur is a first-class real estate investor who teaches investing strategies and methods gleaned from personal experience. Alan has faced many challenges along the way, including having to live in his office for a year. His passion to succeed for the benefit of his family drove him to begin learning real estate investing with whatever free information he could get hold of. This action single-handedly turned his fate around, and led him to create a cash-flow mindset that he shares with his readers and students.

Having "been there and done that," he has expertise developed through pure, "in the trenches" experience. He continues to enrich himself with knowledge, as well as with active investing.

Initially investing in single-family rental homes, he realized he would have to multiply his income source dramatically in order to achieve financial freedom. To that end, he started investing in apartment units.

On the day Alan purchased his first apartment building, he knew he was finally making his dreams a reality. He soon began to earn a "more than comfortable" living through investing. He quit his job and started living the life he always dreamed of—which includes sharing his hard-won know-how with others.

Over the years, he has put together an impressive real estate portfolio and built a company that created jobs for more than 200 employees. Alan and his partners have bought more than 2,000 apartments units, and managed over 7,000 units and hundreds of single-family houses.

Although a force to be reckoned with in the real estate world, he is better known for creating massive amounts of monthly cash flow from his investment properties.

One of his greatest achievements was purchasing an apartment building for $1.25 million that appraised for $4.1 million—instantly creating equity and boosting his net worth.

In a separate transaction, Alan bought an apartment building that continues to bring in over $780,000 in annual income. That's right— $18,000 of cash flow each and every month!

Alan has also founded and sold two companies.

His unique strategies close the gap between investing in single-family properties and apartment units.

CHAPTER 1

THE REAL ESTATE MARKET TODAY

T he days of "buying and flipping" property to make a quick profit are long gone. But, to be honest, this trend was nothing more than a glorified real estate J.O.B. Through the years I've noticed that the most successful real estate entrepreneurs were the ones who concentrated on building massive, passive income. The ones who did not disappear from the investment scene quicker than the chunks of money they made and squandered. Those were the ones who went fleeing back to regular jobs.

Given the state of the real estate market over the past few years, investors and home buyers alike have had to change their strategies for profiting in the market. You could cash flow your dreams using my system. First, though, you must know what your dreams cost and figure out how much you need each month to pay for them!

Many Americans are hard pressed to afford today's still-inflated home prices, especially given our economic upswings and declines. Many are reluctant to make the commitment to buy a home for fear of a further reduction in that home's value and being stuck paying a mortgage on a property that is worth less than the loan amount that is due.

But the good news is ...

Although the real estate market is cyclical—even wildly so—many of these cycles can be profitable if you invest in the right properties, with the right strategies, at all times.

Those millions of homeowners who lost their homes to foreclosure in 2009-2012, as well as the millions of others who simply can't—or won't—purchase a home in the near future, still need some place to live. Apartments fit the bill perfectly!

Whether for those unable to come up with a down payment for a home, those who fear a reduction in home values or those who simply are not in the market to purchase at the moment, apartments provide great value and quality living for many.

Trillions of dollars in the apartment housing business need to be refinanced over the coming years. The sad fact is that much of it won't be. I have seen buildings stripped of core physical assets, such as copper wire by scrappers, and also of equity that appreciated over the past 50 years. This presents a huge opportunity and massive wealth transfer to the real estate apartment entrepreneur.

You have the opportunity to build a legacy not just for you and your family, but for your grandchildren and their families. We have not seen this kind of low pricing in apartment buildings in decades. The perfect time to get involved in real estate is now!

Ask yourself: If you always wanted to get involved in real estate but don't act now, then when will you act? Don't be fooled like so many, and jump in at the top of the market cycle. Focus on your cash flow and use the following information to create wealth. This is not a manual just about getting rich; it's about the accumulation of cash flowing assets that appreciate over time . . . true wealth!

Profiting in Today's Real Estate Environment

Even with the recent uncertainty in real estate markets, there are still numerous ways to profit, IF you follow a proven system. This book will show you such techniques! "Traditional" models of investing will take you five times as long to achieve the same level of wealth as my method— and that is only if you're ambitious.

Using my system, the cash flow that took me five years to accumulate in single-family houses was created within just one year by buying apartment buildings! Not all apartment buildings will return 40 to 80 percent cash-on-cash in one year, but it's not impossible—I have seen it happen.

One apartment building can change your life.

Think about how you will feel, when you are making the same amount of money, as well as building your net worth, in less than a year! This is the main reason that people use my system: to create quantum wealth in order to make up for time lost on traditional, out-of-date models. Part of this process is rebuilding your balance sheet net worth, as well as rebuilding your belief system. If you can break away from the stale ideas that have kept you in your job for years, and grasp the concepts in this book, you could find yourself renting your units to the replacements at your OLD JOB!

CHAPTER 2

THE BIG PICTURE: WHY APARTMENT BUILDINGS AND THE ADVANTAGES OF MULTIFAMILY OWNERSHIP

People often ask me, "How do I get from where I am (usually with investments in single-family homes or just a retirement account) to dealing in larger scale properties such as apartment buildings?" This question typically is followed by a recital of how the investor has tried, without success, to purchase a larger property, or is unsure of the steps necessary to acquire larger, income-producing apartments. Some have not completed their first real estate investment deal and wonder if they could enter commercial real estate without first acquiring smaller properties.

The truth is that many investors start their career by purchasing a single rental home, then another, and maybe a duplex or small apartment building. Sooner or later, they "hit the wall" when they are told by their bank that they can't qualify for any more single-family mortgages, or that their portfolio is outside the bank's lending limits.

This scenario is very common, and unfortunately, is a real problem when it comes to building your real estate property portfolio. Essentially, the investor has gotten too big to deal with the residential lending folks, and is a fish out of water when it comes to knowing how to approach the commercial side of the bank. At that point, you're forced to make a decision about your real estate investing career.

Another concern of many beginning real estate investors is balancing a job while launching a new career. I can tell you from my own experience: It's easy to buy and manage houses while holding down a job. I bought and managed 50 houses while working full time. A multimillion-dollar apartment building might need more of your attention than just a house. Most of us "weekend warriors" who own rental houses work on them after hours. Just keep in mind that while apartment buildings are viewed as more glamorous, most interactions are with professionals who work 9 to 5, Monday through Friday.

Another typical situation is an investor who comes across an apartment complex deal and assumes an existing mortgage or negotiates financing with the seller. If the property proves to be a winner, the investor makes a nice profit and cash flows well, so they go out to look for another deal.

At that point, the flip side of beginner's luck—what I call the "sophomore jinx"—begins to kick in. What seemed so easy with the first property is suddenly proving much more difficult to reproduce. Only then do we have to ask questions that weren't necessary the first time, such as:

- How do I know how much it's worth?
- How do I know the seller is telling me the truth about the cash flow?
- How can it be financed?
- How do I raise the money for the down payment?

The uncertainty of the proposition can be overwhelming.

The book you are holding in your hands will answer all of these questions, and so many more. The answers will help ensure you that you are on the right track, even if investing in apartment buildings for the first time.

Before discussing the "how's" of the transaction, it is important to understand "why" apartment buildings are such sound investments, regardless of your experience level. After all, it has often been said that once you understand the "why," then the "how" is much easier to achieve.

The Benefits of Apartment Buildings over Single-Family Homes and Why You Need to Keep Growing

There are numerous reasons why investing in apartment buildings can be much more beneficial to you than investing in individual, single-family homes. Although at first it might seem overwhelming, investing in these types of properties can be easier in many respect—yet much more profitable due to economies of scale and, simply put, more cash flow within walking distance!

Everybody Needs a Place to Live

One of the biggest reasons to invest in any type of residential real estate is that everybody needs a place to live. As a seasoned business owner, I have learned a very simple lesson: Don't reinvent the wheel! The population in the United States is not shrinking, and neither is the need for commodities across the world. Apartments always provide a much more affordable housing option. My apartments rent from $400 to $1,500 a month, or as little as $13 a day (about 50 cents an hour) for a one-bedroom unit.

In any case, even with a slowing economy and business cutbacks, there always will be demand for your property. In fact, right now, demand for rental property has never been higher. Experts say that over the next decade, rentals will be propelled by the growing number of "eco-boomers," the 18- to 34-year-old children of the baby boomer generation.

This segment of the population alone is estimated to grow nationwide to nearly 73 million by the year 2020. Along with these younger renters, the growing population of senior citizens also will continue to depend on rental housing as a less expensive and less burdensome alternative to home ownership.

Regular Cash Flow

Cash flow (the owner's net spendable income, not to be confused with taxable income), is the lifeblood of any business. The old saying that "Cash is king," is especially true in real estate. Cash flow can be positive, meaning that there is cash left over after paying expenses. Cash flow also can be negative, meaning that not enough revenue is being generated to pay expenses and debt service. Negative cash flow is the worst enemy of every real estate investor.

Forced Appreciation

Along with good, steady cash flow, another benefit to owning apartment buildings is that most complexes can raise their rents annually. This is called "market rents." As rent amounts go up and net income increases, the value of the building also rises. Forcing appreciation on an apartment building can be as simple as decreasing operating expenses or increasing income from rents.

This also helps increase equity, because as tenants continue to essentially pay your mortgage every year, the loan amount decreases and your equity continues to rise until the mortgage is completely paid off. Some of the most successful people I've met in the housing business own their buildings free and clear! Imagine if you could "steal the deal" by finding an apartment complex selling for half of what it's worth—you could own it in half the time, free and clear!

I learned an important lesson a long time ago. If you can figure out how to pay down your properties in good times, you can structure your payments differently in bad times. You can change with the market and always be prepared.

Leverage: How to Get to Here from There

One night, I noticed that a picture of my single-family houses, when I held it sideways, resembled an apartment building. Not just any building, but one I had lived in, in New York City. When I compared this house to the 34-unit building I owned, I realized something else. The units in the apartment building only cost around $13,000 each. And not only were they all in one spot, but they provided a more pleasant business experience and most of all, they were cash flowing as much as my single-family houses!

Most of my single-family houses were purchased for between $30,000 and $50,000 each, or three times more per unit. When I bought the 34-unit building, I learned a lesson that had been right in front of my eyes for 20 years. My cash-on-cash return was much less on the houses compared to these units. *Voila!* That's the gap between single-family houses and apartment buildings. It took me over 10 years to buy 100 houses; it took a single transaction to buy an apartment building with more units, more income and more cash flow!

Ask yourself: Would you rather own 34 individual, single-family homes, or a 34-unit apartment building? With 34 single-family homes, you would need to obtain 34 different mortgages, mow 34 lawns, take care of 34 roofs, and worry about 34 different locations. Overseeing multiple properties in multiple areas could become a logistical nightmare. But with just one 34-unit apartment building, you would have just one mortgage loan, with just one yard and (in most cases) one roof to take care of. You would have just one location to be concerned with, and often, you could hire a property manager to take care of everything.

With multiple properties, of course, you will also have numerous utility bills, tax bills and property insurance premiums. You will also have numerous turnovers or make-readies in different locations, different tax bills, and numerous property insurance premiums. Still, an apartment building gives you the advantage of spreading out the cost of maintaining and paying for the property across more units.

In addition to maintenance, management and expense issues, there is the consideration of selling. When it comes to selling your investment, would you rather have 34 individual properties to put on the market, or just one, single apartment building? Of course, one transaction is the way to go! Leverage with apartment buildings may also mean you have an easier time getting financed through lenders. Even as the sub-prime residential mortgage market has crumbled, banks are still quite eager to loan money on good apartment buildings. Many local banks are wonderful loan providers today because larger banks are still trying to decipher the mess they created over the last decade.

For example, let's say you use $100,000 in cash to purchase a $400,000 apartment building with a $300,000 mortgage, and the property increases in value by $12,000 after one year. That is a 3 percent increase in value, but a 12 percent increase on your $100,000 investment.

Management
Along with leveraging your cost and maintenance, you can also leverage your management expenses with apartment buildings. Many investors

do not want to be property managers—and with good reason. This task tends to take up a great deal of time, especially if you own multiple properties or units.

Trading time for money is not what real estate entrepreneurs do. You can't put a price on your time, and even if you tried, you would eventually run out of both money and time. In other words, you wouldn't be focused on the cash flow.

Don't work for the real estate; make the real estate work for you!

By hiring a third-party property management company, I was able to concentrate more of my time on attracting capital and finding apartment buildings. When first starting out, most real estate entrepreneurs think they can't afford to hire management. But remember: The quicker you free up your time to find the next deal, the better off your portfolio will be.

I can't stress enough that you must do your due diligence when finding a reputable property management outfit, and call references on anyone you select to manage your real estate. To mix metaphors, you could say I have kissed a lot of frogs over the years and run into a few wolves in sheep's clothing. Make sure there is easy separation language in your agreements to use in case the relationship is unsuccessful.

Build the cost of property management into your purchase price and business model. If you buy a small apartment building of less than 34 units, it would require some of your time. You then need to scale up fast to buy more units so that you would be able to pay for quality property management. Sometimes you can combine apartment buildings! I bought a 34- and a 52-unit building and had one manager run both properties.

By taking the necessary steps to hire a good, competent apartment building manager, however, you get to enjoy all the perks of apartment building ownership while leveraging off of somebody else's day-to-day work. It is great to be able to reap all the benefits of ownership—including cash flow, appreciation and tax advantages—without having to do the work of maintaining the property or even collecting rent. Again, if the arrangement is working, great! If not, find the management company the works best for you.

Tax-Shelter and Inflation Fighter

Along with cash flow and the benefits of leveraging, as the owner of an apartment building, you not only can pocket thousands of dollars annually, but you can write off the depreciation, the mortgage interest and the capital expenses, often on a much larger scale than with single-family homes. This has turned out to be a fantastic balance between passive income, write-offs and time. Here, the government is your partner. It wants to incentivize housing investors, but does not want to be in the housing business. This is why some of the best tax breaks are offered in this area.

Apartments also help in the fight against inflation, because rental rates tend to move upward with construction cost increases. Rental leases typically are also adjusted upwards every year, giving you more buying power from the increase in income received.

In addition, apartments can be classified as hard assets, and having your money in hard assets during inflationary times can be very advantageous. Your building is basically a basket of commodities: steel, concrete, wood, land and so on. The world is competing for these very resources. It takes more dollars to buy these resources now than it did in the past. Others fear that too much spending on government programs, economic waste and the devaluation of the U.S. dollar would drive up inflation. I saw this first hand while living in South America. Condos that cost $100,000 skyrocketed to $300,000 during periods of inflation, civil unrest and devaluation of currency.

While inflation moves slower here at home, it does creep up on us.

This means that investing in apartment buildings can also help to hedge against economic volatility. In case of a real estate market downturn, it is possible that you could lower your rental rates to keep your building occupied. When the economy improves, you could always raise the rent again to receive higher cash flows.

Another useful idea is apartment banking, which is when a buyer puts more cash into a purchase in order to pay less in monthly payments to the bank. If you could pay cash for an apartment building in this market, not only would you save tens of thousands in closing costs, but you would also cash flow another 7 to 10 percent a year on your apartment building—a significant amount.

Many successful real estate entrepreneurs leave cash in their deals because they would rather make another healthy return on their money than just leave it in the bank. But I ask, why pay the bank when you can pay yourself? If a better opportunity arises, you could simply refinance.

LESS COMPETITION . . . Don't Be Part of the "Should Have" Group

Investing in apartment buildings also gives you another competitive edge – less competition in the market to purchase these properties. This is because most real estate investors limit their potential by buying properties that require conventional financing. Many times I would go to my local investment club and find that less than 2 percent of real estate investors owned apartment buildings. They seek property based on the amount of funds that they have available, and in most cases, this limits them to single-family properties. Because most investors are looking for single-family homes, you will eliminate the majority of the competition that you'd have with other investors in the market for property. I also have found that apartment buildings worth $4 million or less have much less competition among buyers. A lot of the larger REITS or institutional buyers tend to purchase larger complexes.

Unlike other types of investments, apartment buildings work "overtime" for you. What does this mean, exactly? Well, these investments are working 24 hours a day, seven days a week. Given this, apartment buildings essentially can be considered four investments wrapped into one. These are the type of investments we need if we are going to get ahead. As the world increasingly becomes more of a single, global economy, you will need more aggressive methods to pay for your lifestyle. Most people want the same things in life and are willing to work for much less. The average person makes $2 a day in this world! When some of these people arrive to the United States, they are hungry and ready to work hard. But, many investors use outdated methods that were taught decades ago. That's why 95 percent of people in this world die broke. If you take the time to build an apartment portfolio with a cash flow mindset, the apartment complex will take care of you.

To succeed, especially in the apartment business. it's important to do the right thing at the right time. It's important to identify your current markets and make the right investment decisions to create an incredible cash flowing future.

The Bottom Line: How Do You Make a Profit?

First, understand that the property—if purchased and sold correctly—will increase in value. The benefits of apartment ownership could help you avoid years of unnecessary work!

Second, while you are holding the property, tenants' rental income will provide you with regular, monthly cash flow. Therefore, even before you sell the property, provided your expenses are below the total incoming rent, you will earn a regular monthly income, as well.

Third, owning an apartment building will allow you to claim depreciation against earned income on your taxes. (Please consult with your tax planner regarding your specific situation.)

Last—but certainly not least—Uncle Sam allows you to sell your property and defer paying any taxes on the sale for as long as you want. In fact, apartments are one of the few investments that, when sold, allow you to roll over all of your capital gains taxes from the sale into your next investment and legally defer all of those taxes. This is otherwise known as a 1031 IRS exchange. Again, consult with your accountant on how this would affect your situation.

So, you can certainly see how, within a very short time, your profits could truly begin to add up after you invest in apartment buildings. This is the basic idea behind the system you will learn in this book: how to use leverage repeatedly to keep your profit momentum going.

There are many advantages to investing in apartment buildings. Using the system outlined here, your potential for profit can come in as little as three to 18 months, a much shorter time frame than those offered by most "traditional" investments. These are some of the choices I made early in my career that proved to be the right choices.

Profiting within a shorter time provides you the potential to grow your overall profits—and your net worth—at a much faster pace than is possible using a typical "buy and hold" method. Doing this also lets you enjoy the fruits of your labor much sooner so that you can retire young and healthy and keep building your fortune, or pursue other dreams.

Some of the distinct advantages I found with investing in apartment buildings:

- Lower cost per unit than single-family homes.
- Greater cash-on-cash return.
- Great demand for apartments, especially considering the fore-closure crises that tend to affect us in the United States. Many of us experienced the downturn of housing markets around 2010. Crashes like this, and fear of future downturns, make it harder for younger families to take the plunge and purchase a home, so they often stay mobile and prefer the option of renting an apartment.
- The possibility of instant profitability, due to the positive cash flow already in place. In some cases, depending upon the property, this positive cash flow could be enough to replace your current income, allowing you to quit your job and live off the income stream from the investment.
- Relying on a competent property manager so you never have to worry about fixing toilets, waiting for repairmen, or dealing with tenants.
- Financing, in many cases, is easier to obtain for apartment buildings than other forms of real estate.
- Apartment buildings typically appreciate faster than single-family houses—especially where there is strong demand in metropolitan areas.
- Numerous tax benefits.

Let's get into the details so you can see how this system could boost both your short- and long-term profits by maximizing your leverage and investing in apartment buildings.

CHAPTER 3

FINDING THE GREAT DEALS AND GETTING INSPIRED

I f you get nothing else from this book, I hope you will understand the greatest, hidden source of the best deals ever found: the concept of receivership. It's not exactly a new idea in corporate America, but it's becoming very popular in commercial real estate and, especially, with apartment complexes.

Let me explain.

Some unsuccessful apartment operators are put into default by the lender. The lender is unhappy with the way the owner is running the project or building. Next, you have the lender that goes through a traditional process to gain control of the property, but without getting their name on the property, because this is a huge liability for lenders. They don't want to take responsibility for these properties because they don't want to be involved with a potentially large lawsuit. They never intended one from the owner, either.

So what do they do? They go to a judge, who appoints a receiver. Who is a receiver? Well, in most cases, the receiver is a property management company who then runs the building.

But here's the golden nugget in all of this: The receiver slowly strips the owner of all their rights, including millions and millions of dollars of equity. In 2017, there are literally billions of dollars that need to be refinanced and that might lead to more receivership possibilities for investors.

For example, I bought a 72-unit apartment building through this scenario. Problems began, believe it or not, with a growing colony of bats! The owner, Sam, couldn't believe it, either—and didn't do anything about it. Bats ended up driving this building out of business because the city came in and got very upset. The complex had to be evacuated.

The result? An empty building that can't afford to pay the bills. The bank takes it back through receivership. This is where I came into the story. Scott, my broker, called me up and said, "Hey Alan! There's a bank in Minnesota that owns this property in Lake Jackson, Texas. They want to get rid of it at any price!"

I drove the 50 or so miles from Houston to Lake Jackson the next day. We're on top of the apartment building, inspecting the roofs. Scott looks at me and says, "Hey, Alan! I know you just bought a 162-unit complex. But I'm telling you, you're going to make more money on this 72-unit complex than that one."

He was right! Why?

Check this out. I bought the complex for $1.125 million (purchase statement). It appraised for over $4 million! As you can see, the equity capture here is huge. How many transactions for single-family homes would you have to do to capture that kind of equity? With apartment buildings, the number is just one! It didn't take long at all. At that point, I was hooked!

Best of all—I have to tell you—this building reached monthly cash flow of $24,000 within my first four months of ownership. Could you imagine how much an extra $24,000 could help your bottom line? These are the deal changers— the golden eggs I want you to hold onto when you find them. These are the apartment buildings that we're looking for that can create a legacy for you and your family, free up your time and give you the financial freedom to do whatever you want to do.

I'm doing really well with receivership deals and bank deals, and have a few recommendations for others. Get to know a commercial broker in your hometown. They know where the great deals are. Don't just use your single-family house broker. Take the time to form a new relationship. Foster that relationship and get on your broker's A-list so that you are the absolute first phone call they make when an incredible deal comes up.

One time, I purchased a 160-unit building for $720,000. It sold for $3 million two years ago in a bank foreclosure receivership deal, and I was the first person my broker called. But you have to devote the time and energy to build that kind of relationship. It's simple, and will ensure your economic future. There is a saying that your network is your net worth. Start hanging out with the right people, and spend far less time with the "wrong" ones.

Win-Win Funding Using Little or No Money Down

I constantly hear comments like this: "Hey Alan, I wasn't born with a silver spoon in my mouth." Or, "I don't have $500,000 to invest, but want to get started. How can I get in with little or no money down?"

I tell them all that every self-made millionaire started off with nothing, too.

I actually have dozens of strategies, but let's focus on just a few right now.

A common term for the many different ways you can combine strategies to raise money is "capital stack." Money partners are a great way of raising funds. You will need to make a decision: Will your partners simply lend money in exchange for a return? Or, will you give them equity in the deal, too? These partners are very important. What do they bring? Money, expertise and their own networks of friends and associates. Some of them have introduced me to strategies for funding apartment deals, while others have used traditional financing with bankers. I once had a partner who used a master lease option to buy a property while he continued to run and cash flow the property, with no money down. A master lease option is when the seller lets the buyer use his financing and they agree on a future date and option to purchase the property.

Always Stress That This Is a Collaboration!

If you can find a seller-financed deal and only need a small down payment, why not borrow private money from your partner? They don't want equity in the deal, but rather, just a return on their money.

Substitution of collateral partners can be very useful, too. Sometimes our partners are not liquid with cash, but have lots of equity locked up in other investments. Many banks will let your partners post their property for collateral and lend on your existing project.

A few months ago, I had to decide whether to go to an afternoon classes hosted by my local investment club, or attend a PTA meeting with my wife. I'm sure a lot of you know which one I chose.

I picked a seat in the audience at random, and ended up meeting Pat. What can I say? You can find terrific, knowledgeable people at your local investment clubs.

Once you are producing not just incremental gains, but exponential gains, year after year, investors will come looking for you. At that point, it's time to push yourself to become the best at what you do—the best promoter, the Bentley of your field. I believe you can do it!

Money Follows Management

Another method of raising money is a **Private Placement Memorandum**, or PPM. This is my preferred method of raising funds and working with new partners. This very powerful method pools partners to raise funds.

This is truly the game changer. I no longer find myself sitting at Starbucks or my kitchen table, pitching a deal to somebody in an attempt to raise money. Now, we meet at Starbucks, and we'll have coffee, talk about the family, and what's new and exciting out there. Then, I'll say, "Oh, by the way, here's a private placement memorandum." A PPM is a 75- to 100-page document written by an attorney with the U.S. Securities and Exchange Commission (SEC), and it explains the rules and regulations, as well as the numbers and facts you'd need to know in order to raise money through this kind of deal. The documents are very clear regarding what each person should expect from the deal.

When you put these private placement memorandums together, you can collect money for acquisition fees; you can collect money on rehab overrides and construction overrides; you get to collect money on exit strategies; and you get to collect money on cash flow.

I would recommend using an SEC attorney to create the documents for the apartment complex you want to buy before raising funds using this strategy.

So remember: Partner up when you don't need the money, because when you find yourself in a position when timing is important, people tend to hold onto their money and respond much more slowly. It's like an insurance policy, in that you can't buy one after you need it!

As for equity partners, they want to own a piece of your apartment deal. It's that simple. In my deals that I promote, I offer a combination of both equity ownership and a return of interest on my partner's money, so they have a piece of the whole deal—both the profit and the losses. They are there for paychecks.

Debt partners, on the other hand, just want a rate of return. They are non-owners and are not looking for a job, but just the return on their capital and of their capital! Remember to use legal agreements (and create a PPM) in these deals, and have an exit strategy ready before entering the deal.

Other Things I Like to Look for that Mean Great Buys:

- 50 percent or higher vacancy, which indicates tenant problems
- A run-down apartment complex in a great location
- Eligibility for grants, tax credits or municipal incentives
- Huge traffic count with the opportunity to rent out signage
- New public works projects in the area
- Sellers offering creative terms or seller financing
- Long hold periods, such as a "100 percent depreciated property" (indicating seller problems)
- Flippers
- Mismanaged assets
- Poor landscaping

Seller Carry-Back Notes

Partners and creative financing have been very valuable to me, as well. One of my favorite strategies is seller carry-back notes. These allow the seller to lower the price of the apartment building and help you obtain new financing by putting a part of the equity into a second note payment.

This allows you to get the financing you need from the lender, because you need to borrow less. Other times, properties will not appraise for the value that you or the seller need them to. I have witnessed sellers agree to a lower price, but create seller carry-back financing to close the deal. But be careful! Don't over leverage. Remember, as the buyer, you will need to make two payments if you get the money: one to the seller, and the other to the bank.

Owner financing is invaluable if you need to raise capital. This is another great way of getting into a deal with little or no money down. I have been in a few situations when the property didn't appraise for enough to qualify to receive all the funds from the bank. In these cases, the owner can make up the difference by placing a lien on the property so that you can purchase it. Just make sure you can make both payments to the seller.

This reminds me of a story. One time I was sitting down with Mike, an investor in my deal. He looked at me, perplexed, as I was raising money. He said, "Alan, this looks incredible. But in three months, you're going to have no money in this deal, with all the money that you're making for the deal." And he was absolutely right! I found the deal, brought a group of investors together, and used the PPM, so I was in this deal for no money down. But I'm going to get 30 percent across the board for running the deal, and I explained to Mike how this was an unbelievable opportunity for everyone. It truly was, since we both made 30 percent profit when I sold the deal a year later.

Every Investor Wants To Know: What Will Be My Cash-On-Cash Return?

This always seems to be the first question I hear after presenting a great real estate deal. Be sure you know who you are speaking to. Be clear on who your target investor is so that you don't waste your time. Any savvy real estate investor can recognize a good deal. Just know what they are looking for. Most likely, they have choices on where they invest. So, the question in their mind becomes, Why should I invest with you? What makes you the best choice for them at this particular time? From experience, I can tell you to be honest, tell the story and let them know that you respect their money and will be a good steward of the fruits of their hard-won effort. Explain to them how you will provide regular reports on the property, and how they can further engage with you.

Characteristics of Commercial Properties

Numerous property types are associated with apartment buildings, and they vary a great deal in the way they are operated and managed. Although this variety can help investors tailor particular investments to their specific wants and needs, sorting through the myriad choices can be somewhat confusing.

Once you realize that there are many alternatives, you will be able to narrow down your choice of building to one that closely aligns with your individual talents, resources and goals as an investor.

Letter grades—something like the old star ratings for hotels—are commonly used to describe the different types of commercial properties in the market. It is important to note that even though a property may be an "A" property, or a "B" property in an "A" location, a property's overall grade will refer to its relative quality as measured against other properties in the same market.

Although there is no specific standard for the use of the actual terms, the investment community typically assigns letter rankings according to three criteria: the property's location, the strength of the property's tenants, and the physical condition of the property itself, including its age. This provides something akin to a barometer, and with some ratios, you can compare properties across the United States. Once you learn just 10 or 20 of the most important things, you can master this whole system to create a legacy for everybody you care about—including yourself.

A Class Properties

A class properties are in the top tier in the market, with prime locations, strong and stable rent rolls, and buildings that are in excellent physical condition and constructed with high-quality materials. The exteriors typically are well landscaped. In most cases, A properties were built within the last 10 years.

These also are the highest-priced properties because, typically, institutional investors (such as pension funds, insurance companies or REITs) want these properties in their portfolios and will bid up the price.

B Class Properties

B class properties are in good-to-great locations and have a good rent roll. While there might be few vacancies with B properties, the tenants might not be as desirable as those in an A property. They might also have older leases, with near-term expiration dates of less than three years.

In addition, while the buildings are typically in good condition, in most cases the structure is usually older and in need of at least some repair. In general, B properties were built within the last 20 years. Similarly, the amenity package might be somewhat dated and offer less than properties in the A category.

C Class Properties

C class properties typically will need some immediate attention to get back up to par. Their locations, once deemed desirable, typically have deteriorated and become a poor place to own property. They generally will have a high tenant turnover, as well as rent collection problems. The vacancy rate is usually higher than the normal rate of about 15 percent.

The physical infrastructure will nearly always require significant maintenance, often including the replacement of major systems such as roofs, heating and cooling systems, and electrical or plumbing. Typically, C properties were built within the last 30 years.

Despite these issues, C properties often are terrific turnaround properties that offer high profit potential to an investor who is willing to commit the time and effort needed to fix them up. If neglected, however, C properties end up in the lowest letter ranking.

D Class Properties

These properties—the true dogs of the real estate world—are often promoted as being priced "below replacement cost." They are in bad locations and have very few (or very weak) tenants who usually are in short-term leases of less than one year, or who rent month to month.

These properties generally are more than 30 years old and have many major physical problems, including poor design and/or significant structural deficiencies. Unfortunately, these factors usually cannot be profitably overcome.

The lesson is this: always be planning for the future. If you buy a property today, ask yourself what type of asset it will be in a few years. Could your B property slide into the C category? Your strategy for either repositioning or maintaining the property should be crystal clear.

How can you leverage this knowledge? By starting small (or medium). You can make money, and sometimes much more money, from C or D class buildings than A or B class buildings.

Real Estate Nugget

Here's a quick story.

At the beginning of 2011, I bought a C class building for $16,000 per unit. Within a few years, monthly cash flow was $22,000! I have one partner in the deal, so it generated $11,000 for me. We made some minor changes to the property that bumped it up a class. Along with that came a lot of extra income.

Locating Properties and Finding Great Deals

You will learn that ads can be misleading, and not every property listed as A class actually is in top condition. The only way to tell for sure is by thoroughly inspecting the property yourself, or through a professional property inspector. I have walked many C properties that were purely D. I also have walked through many C's that—happily for me—turned out to be B's.

It's hard to reposition or raise a property's class by more than one level. For example, I have bought C class buildings, raised their rents, and fixed them up to B class standards, but never achieved any higher. Be careful to not over spend. Make sure that the market rents support your reinvestment.

CHAPTER 4

WHAT MAKES AN INVESTMENT PROFITABLE

H ere's what you're not being told about apartment buildings: Analyzing them is not that difficult!

Many investors who buy apartment buildings have experience in other areas of real estate investing (typically, single-family homes and duplexes). It seems that the primary issue facing investors who are entering the apartment building niche is the fact that these properties are valued using different methods than those of residential real estate. If we know how to read, interpret and measure our financials, our success rate will increase dramatically.

For example, commercial real estate investors can use a variety of appraisal methods to determine the fair market value of an apartment building. These methods should not be intimidating to new investors. Once you understand them, they can help you to locate the very best match for your real estate investing goals.

Although there is a wide variety of investment choices on the market today—many of which have some very appealing features—it always is best to make investment decisions with full knowledge of all the ramifications.

First and foremost, investors need to understand what produces good real estate investment returns. The five factors we will explore here are cash flow, tax benefits, equity growth, capital appreciation and capitalization rate.

You need to have systems in place to manage and measure your costs so you know how much you're making. When all else fails and the numbers don't make sense, just walk away from the deal. Finding a formula that works for you will make you rich.

Cash flow refers to the funds that are available after the payment of operating expenses and debt payments. In its most basic sense, your pretax cash flow is calculated as gross income minus operating expenses and debt service.

One factor that can have a huge impact on cash flow is debt per door, or how much money you borrowed to buy the apartment unit compared to the number of units. If you are an expert running an extraordinarily well-tuned machine and you're doing everything you're supposed to be doing, then the equation comes down to debt per door.

Here's a really good example. I bought a foreclosure for $4,300 a door. Insanely cheap! Soon after that, my biggest competitor in the area paid $25,000 a door two blocks away. He has to service his building debt at approximately $25,000 a door. All I have to do is run my building just as well as he does (or better) and service my debt at less than one quarter that amount per door—a no-brainer.

I realized that if I kept my debt per door low, I might even be able to charge as much rent as the person who paid $25,000 a door by poaching his best tenants. I truly had the best product at the best price. I picked the low-hanging fruit from the trees, cleaned up the building, and cleaned up the neighborhood. I kept the debt so low that the property became extremely profitable. I have apartment buildings cash flowing 80 percent cash-on-cash per year right now because I bought them very cheaply and their debt per door is extremely low.

The best time for investors to determine whether an investment property will have a positive cash flow is before buying it. The idea of generating positive cash flow helps investors ensure that their returns on a particular investment will be greater than if they had not invested the cash at all, or if it were put in an alternate investment. This is typically referred to as cash-on-cash return. The larger the return on the cash invested, the better the investment.

Certainly, positive cash flow is a very effective way to invest in real estate, and especially in apartment buildings that have the potential to generate high cash flow. Therefore, knowing how to calculate cash-on-cash return is the key to determining your potential profit from a particular investment.

When looking at apartment buildings, the unit mix is a very important consideration. I like two-bedroom units more than one-bedrooms. In a 100-unit building, I would prefer a mix of 60/40. Two-bedroom apartments tend to cater more to families who typically stay longer than tenants who rent one-bedrooms.

Job Growth Keeps Your Apartment Complexes Full

I also try to find out as much as I can about the local economy that I'm buying into, and you should, too. Job growth is one of the main drivers that will help you succeed in the real estate business. The more growth in the area, the better off the community and its residents will be. If large corporations are investing to your area, then you should be, as well.

I like to find small towns that are 10 to 20 miles from major cities experiencing explosive job growth (otherwise known as tertiary or secondary markets). In these towns, there is usually not much new construction, nor is there a shortage of apartments. We find that if a major city is growing fast, we can find a better-value deal a few towns over. I currently own one complex in an area that is adding thousands of jobs due to business expansion. Local banks in the area like to invest in their backyards and might get credit from the government for investing in their community, too.

Replacement Riches and Rebuilding Costs

Knowing the replacement cost of the apartment building is important. This will affect the price of the insurance you will need to purchase. I own many buildings that I purchased for less than half of what they are insured for.

I also know people who made millions of dollars after storms or fires destroyed their buildings. Hurricane Ike—the third-costliest Atlantic hurricane, causing $25 billion in damage—wiped out many apartment owners on Galveston Island, about 50 miles southeast of Houston, when it hit the Texas Gulf Coast in 2008. The owners had bought, at a huge discount, class C and D properties that were 30 to 40 years old. While the hurricane blew away older structures, the insurance policies had to pay replacement costs (including ensuring that the new structures met all modern building codes) to prevent future devastation. In short, complexes that had been purchased for $1 or $2 million were now worth $5 or $6 million. The owners took the money, paid off the original mortgage and pocketed the difference. The lesson: Always insure, because storms can make you a (literal) windfall!

In some cases, even poorly managed apartment buildings have hidden potential for generating income. Sprucing up the property's curb appeal, adding amenities or even launching a more effective marketing campaign can help bring in top rental dollars, as well as other potential income streams.

Older properties should be inspected to identify any hidden short- or medium-term expenses, such as a roof replacement or issues regarding the building's structural integrity that may not be obvious.

In addition, investors must remember to accurately budget for regular upkeep expenses, as well as any potential unexpected repairs or replacements. Maintenance issues lead to tenant complaints, so it is important to pay especially close attention as problems arise. Keep in mind that prevention is much less expensive than a cure, and ignoring maintenance could have a significant, negative effect your property's bottom line. I use software that is offered for free on my website to help analyze apartment deals.

Tax Benefits

Two types of cash flow, when combined, can create a mountain of wealth: actual cash flow and phantom cash flow. Knowing about them can make you rich or poor, and can save you years of unnecessary work as you speed up your wealth creation process.

When used properly, my real estate method will help you find more time to do the things you want. Part of that comes with understanding how taxes and working with accountants can get you ahead in the wealth game.

A property can have a positive cash flow yet still generate a "paper loss" for tax purposes. Gains on a property investment can also be tax deferred. For example, you can take a piece of real estate, fix it up and then trade it, basically sell it, roll your money into another piece of real estate, and not pay capital gains at all.

If you choose to sell your apartment building and buy a larger one, a very advantageous way to do so is through an instant wealth builder called a 1031 exchange (also referred to as a deferred exchange). I wish somebody had explained this to me when I was 18 years old. I think I would have created a different plan for myself. It's such a powerful technique. I like to compare it to an IRA, Roth or other retirement plan because it allows you to pyramid up and explode your wealth. The idea is that your cash flow will grow out of tax-deferred money that would have otherwise left you. Instead, you own more units with more cash flow coming in from each one.

For example, you follow my directions and buy a 12-unit building for 20 to 30 cents on the dollar. You stabilize it, you do everything you're supposed to do, and you're cash flowing it. On the street, your building appears to be a regular asset, like all the others. Then, maybe, the time comes to sell it, because people are looking for really great returns right now, after getting just 0 to 1 percent.

You've created something that returns a good 10 to 30 percent annually, and people will pay a lot of money for that. So, if you pay $100,000 for something and sell it for, let's say, $300,000, you'd typically have a $200,000 capital gain if you sold it within the first year. You can simply roll all of that gain, tax-free, into the next property. Tax-free, that is, until you die.

The most powerful result of this entire process is the cash flow. Your apartment portfolio keeps getting larger and better while you are profiting and cash flowing off of all that captured equity that you never have to pay taxes on in the first place. It has been a traditional path for somebody to go from owning five or 10 units to owning 5,000 or 10,000 units. It's an unbelievable technique—the sky's the limit, and you don't pay taxes on the money for a long time, perhaps even forever! I have met people who began with 12 units and accumulated 10,000. That's how a lot of big, wealthy companies do it. They're selling these apartment buildings, making millions of dollars tax-free, and then rolling that right back into a bigger asset, creating more returns for their investors.

1031 Exchange

When using a 1031 exchange, a facilitator takes the cash that comes out of your apartment building sale and holds it until you close escrow on the new property that you are purchasing. That property must be identified within 45 days and must be closed on within six months to take advantage of these tax benefits. The replacement property must also be purchased for more than the price for which you sold your first property. Many investors use this strategy for years as they continue buying larger properties and defer taxes indefinitely.

If, however, you decide to sell your property without using a 1031 exchange, you will pay taxes on the gain. But if you take cash out through refinancing rather than selling your property, those dollars are tax-free until you sell. As long as you continue to hold on to the property, you continue to defer the taxes on those funds.

Management and Operations

Management

My philosophy is simple: Hire the best. Pay them richly, but pay them mostly on performance, and they will always do more than you ask. There is good management and bad. Figure out quick which one you have. If reports starts coming in later than expected or are missing information, this is a red flag that you might have a bad property management company working for you. I have dealt with both the good and the bad in my career. Touring a potential property will help you get a good idea of the situation. As you take notes, remember that the most obvious problems might offer the greatest opportunities for improvement (and improving the return on your investment).

Two of the most common areas of potential improvement that you can jump on right away are management and expansion. When evaluating the current management of a property you are considering, you need to be truly objective in determining exactly what is fixable and what is not. Keep in mind that some problems may not have any viable solutions.

It can be difficult to determine whether poor performance is the result of bad management or an external cause. It is easy to blame the manager for a poorly performing property, but sometimes there are very legitimate reasons that have nothing to do with management.

Remember that a change in management will not improve performance if the market cannot support the product. For instance, poor maintenance and bad property conditions may have left a property with a terrible reputation. Unless the underlying problems are fixed, a change in the front office staff likely will not help. Therefore, a good understanding of the underlying fundamentals of the market position and condition are necessary to make a sound judgment.

Ultimately, whether you manage the property yourself or hire a company, you need to act professionally at all times. Make every effort to collect rents. Maximize filling up your units. Minimize the downtime when turning over units. Maintain the property's physical condition. Keep accurate records of lease agreements, collections, maintenance and all personnel paperwork.

Operations

"Once you build one successful business, you have the skills to build as many as you want." —Alan Schnur

Your word is your bond. Do what you say you will do. Your actions truly reflect your beliefs much more than your words ever could. This, by far, is the axiom that has proven to be true throughout my life. If you're raising capital or running the operation, don't be afraid to roll up your sleeves and get your hands dirty. Most of all, make sure the task at hand gets completed.

Getting your systems and operations under control is a sure path to success. The overall operation of the property itself is the critical factor in profitability. The key factors here are leases, rents, expenses (such as utilities), and how each is handled.

Some of the information that you must evaluate:

- Copies of all leases.
- Rent rolls (current and for the past three years). This should include information on the lease start and end date for each tenant, as well as their rent amount, deposit amount and payment history.
- Concessionary rents.
- Lease expiration report.
- Utility bills and usage information, including water, sewer, gas, electric, cable, Internet and phone (current and past two years).
- Property taxes (current and past three years).
- Service contracts.
- Advertising contracts.
- All employment contracts.
- Payroll register.
- Operating manuals (for phones, computers and so on).
- Insurance (including a comprehensive claim history for the past three years, and carrier risk assessment).
- Management contract.
- Commission agreements.
- Miscellaneous agreements (vending machines, pay phones and so on).
- Capital improvements and maintenance history (past three years).
- Marketing association agreements.
- Yellow Pages listing contract.
- Credit bureau contract.
- Tenant file examination (including applications and leases).
- Pet policy.

Leases, Rent Rolls and Utility Bills
Leases
Leases are the most important documents for owners of income properties. These properties typically are sold subject to all the existing leases.

Therefore, it is extremely important to examine every lease before deciding to buy a property. In addition, these leases must be checked against the rent roll to help verify the property's operating statement.

Building owners often will use a standard lease, modifying certain terms to reflect any agreements with individual tenants for improvements or concessions. These side agreements often are an incentive to get a tenant to sign a lease.

You also will need to check the credit quality of your residential tenants. It cannot be stressed enough that filling property vacancies with sub-par tenants will cost you money in the long run. If your review reveals poor or non-existent credit reports and a lack of tenant references, this could be a red flag.

Do not take the importance of leases lightly, as it will be your job to evict tenants, prepare units for leasing to new tenants, and incur the expense of carrying vacant units until new tenants arrive. If a problem is widespread, your investment very quickly could essentially become a turnaround project.

Rent Rolls

One of the most important documents to request from the current owner of an apartment building as you assess whether to make an offer is the rent rolls. These reports consolidate the information contained in tenant leases. They give the name, apartment number and amount of rent paid by each tenant in the building. By closely inspecting both the current and historical rent rolls, you can obtain a great deal of important information about the property.

Some rent roll reports are more detailed than others, and could even show a tenant's payment history, any outstanding balances and the beginning date of the lease.

It is a good idea to make sure the leases are legitimate and that tenants are actually paying the amount recorded on the rent roll. I like to meet a few of the tenants and match their names on the leases. You can verify the amount paid by finding copies of the cashed checks in the seller's bank account. If the seller seems reluctant to provide the necessary financial information, that might be a sign that you should pass on that particular building and move on to another. A seller that has neglected to maintain accurate financial records is likely to have also skimped in other areas, such as maintenance or management. Again, this is very likely a red flag.

Some sellers also go out of their way to fill up their buildings with undesirable tenants to improve their physical occupancy (the actual number of tenants). This is different from economic occupancy. For example, if you have a 100-unit building and 98 units are rented, your physical occupancy is 98 percent. But if you have collected rent on only 80 units, your economic occupancy is just 80 percent. Be smart here! Ask the right questions. Base your purchasing decision on actual data, not pro formas: 100 units, but only 80 have paid . . . those are the real, hard facts.

Whenever possible, you should review at least three years of rent rolls and compare these figures with whatever financial information you were given by the seller or the seller's real estate broker or agent. Information regarding concessionary rents and lease expiration reports could also be generated from the rent roll or a review of the leases. If the seller supplies reports for your review, this information should be verified.

Another thing to look at is the tenant turnover rate. Unusually high turnover could indicate problems with either the building management or maintenance. Keep in mind that it will cost you money every time you replace a tenant, so a high turnover rate could have a significant impact on your bottom line.

Utility Bills

Utility bills are very important. Utilities often are higher-expense items in operating an apartment complex, and it is important to review and investigate these bills beyond a cursory look at the amounts and expenses reported.

Monthly or annual utility costs as they are shown on a property's operating statement are not enough to solidly determine whether the cost and usage are in line with established norms. It is a good idea to request copies of at least two years' worth of actual monthly utility bills that show both cost and usage.

Obtaining this information should not be difficult. Even if the current property does not have actual copies of these bills, the utilities company could provide them. Some might require that the request come directly from the current property owner. In many cases, you can obtain information that outlines the property's monthly usage, rates and costs for up to the past five years.

The reason you must pay such close attention to utility bills and usage is because utilities have characteristics that are not found in other expenses. First, for example, the use of utilities can fluctuate seasonally, so that monthly statements are necessary for a comparison of equal time periods. Statements that show only annual usage tend to hide areas of overconsumption.

Next, many utility companies bill on a bi-monthly or quarterly basis, rather than monthly. This can make usage and cost comparisons from one year to the next difficult, depending on when the billing cycle hits in the statement period, and the accounting system used for the particular property.

Another reason utility bills are so important is that they can be the only real way to gauge usage by units (such as gallons or watts) on a per-occupied-unit basis. Unless utility usage is analyzed on a per-occupied-unit basis, finding spikes in usage that may indicate abnormal conditions (specifically, leaks and/or system malfunctions) is difficult.

In some cases, however, this information could be matched with historical rent rolls to calculate per-occupied-unit cost and use. If that particular level of detail isn't available for past years, you could essentially estimate the annual occupancy rate to determine the number of occupied apartment units. If the building or property happens to have multiple usage meters, you will need to be sure to match the meter readings with the actual units being served.

In addition, keep in mind that many utility companies are owned and operated by municipal providers. As a result of recent financial stress placed on many local governments, many municipalities have been forced to make their utility operations self-sufficient. Some have even taken the additional step of turning their utility operations into profit centers to generate revenue without having to raise taxes.

You must be careful, therefore, to examine utility bills not only for past cost and usage, but also to monitor the trend in rate increases from the utility companies themselves. This is a very important aspect in projecting your future operating expenses.

In some of our buildings, we offer tenants an all-bills-paid option. We put in a maximum amount of usage, otherwise known as a ceiling price. For example, we give an allowance up to $150 for a one-bedroom apartment. Tenants who exceed that amount are responsible for paying the difference. We receive a commercial rate and in some cases make money on the all-bills-paid option if the tenant doesn't use the allotted amount.

Gas companies have become more deregulated as well. In Houston, for instance, I was able to choose a provider for one of my apartment buildings and in effect save 30 percent of my annual natural gas bill. These savings can have a huge impact on your net operating income (NOI) and are well worth looking into.

Insurance and Personal Property
Insurance Claims History

Once you have examined the information regarding utilities, you must review the property's claims history, since this is attached to the property, not whoever was owner at the time of the claim. Because of this, a property that has made multiple claims could be subject to higher insurance costs going forward. You will need to request from the current property owner information regarding all claims placed on the property. If this information is not readily available, the insurance company or companies will have a record of it.

Capital Improvements

Likewise, you should also request information on any capital improvements the current owner made to the building(s) and overall property. It is a good idea to be aware of any work that has been done, as well as who performed the work and whether there are any outstanding claims or warranties associated with the major systems and structure of the building(s).

The age and warranty status of the roof and the property's HVAC systems are of primary importance. Be sure to note that any warranties still in effect must be transferred to you at the property closing.

Having these warranties transferred is of utmost importance for both property maintenance and financing. Many lenders will inquire about whether there are system warranties, as this helps the lender gauge the capital reserve requirements that might be associated with a new loan. If there is an existing loan on the property with a capital reserve account, arrangements will need to be made to account for any balance in the account at closing.

Personal Property

Along with the financial and physical aspects of the property, you must factor in any associated personal property that will be included in the deal. This is typically dealt with on a case-by-case basis. In some cases, it might not be an essential part of your initial property analysis or make a huge difference in the overall return of the property, but it should at least be analyzed.

It is typically assumed that unit-specific items, such as appliances and other furnishings, will transfer to the new owner. However, it is still necessary to state these details in the sale contract.

Prior to closing on the property, you should conduct an inventory of all major items of personal property. You should provide the closing agent with a copy of this inventory to be included in the bill of sale.

Buyers of larger properties tend to overlook items of personal property that are furnished for tenants, as well as items such as tools, supplies and other equipment used in day-to-day operations. Again, never simply assume that these items will be transferred automatically; this must be stated in writing in the contract. Remember, sewing machines, carpet cleaners and computers are not cheap!

Equity and Capital
Equity Growth

Over the lifetime of a mortgage, debt service payments will amortize (or pay down) the amount of principal due. With apartment buildings, however, this amount is primarily paid down with rent funds received from tenants.

Equity growth is calculated as the property's market value minus the total debt owed on the property. This is not necessarily equal to the amount of capital invested. As a property is held over a longer period of time, the amount of equity usually will increase, assuming normal market conditions with a constant rate of property values.

It is important that you don't confuse equity with a property's book value. Book value is different from both the property's market value and tax-assessed value. Also known as tax basis, book value is the cost basis of the property used for income tax purposes. In general, book value is the cost of the property plus any capitalized improvements and loan costs, minus accumulated depreciation.

A property's book value is used to calculate taxable gain when the property is sold. That gain is determined by subtracting the basis plus the costs of the sale from the sales price. The tax implications of a property sale are important to know and understand because these numbers can make a big difference in your decision to sell or exchange a property.

Over time, the property's book value will decrease as depreciation deductions are taken, unless significant capital improvements are made to replenish the account. It is a good idea to have your accountant keep a running total of the current tax basis of your investment properties, and to regularly review this total.

Capital Appreciation

Capital appreciation is the profits realized upon the resale of a property from the increase in value over the time that the investor held the property. The ultimate yield of an investment is the sum of these returns over the holding period. The investment can be structured to produce more of any one of the returns, or a combination of returns. The timing of the returns can be just as important as the amount.

Leveraging Money

The less money you have in the deal, the more money you will make on your investment. Whether you have limited funds or a few million, the same rule applies. If you could buy a piece of real estate for $100 and aren't required to have a down payment, your return is infinite since it's a no-money-down deal. Technically, you could do as many of these deals as you want without running out of money.

If you made a $10 down payment, then your percentage return would be based off of that $10. If the investment appreciated by a dollar, your return would be a 10 percent return on cash. But if you only had $100 to invest, you could own only 10 of these properties. If you could figure out how to buy the property with nothing down, or how to pull your money out later, you could again own a potentially unlimited amount of real estate. Personally, I've become a master at the process of pulling my money out.

Here is the formula I used to build my first fortune in the real estate business. Remember, it's possible to purchase real estate cheap enough so that when a refinance takes place, you can pull out all of your down payment money, or simply create a larger cash flow for yourself. What is important is that you make the decision about how much cash flow or cash on hand you need.

1. 100 houses worth $100,000 each = $10 million portfolio
2. Paid $40,000 per house with Bank A, then refinanced with Bank B at $50,000 = $5 million debt
3. ROI = Infinite + $1 million in my pocket, tax-free

The result: I own 100 houses, have no cash into the deals, put $1 million in my pocket and have increased my net worth on my balance sheet by $5 million.

Capitalization Rate

A property's capitalization (or cap) rate reflects the return that you would receive over one year if your investment property had been purchased fully in cash. When you apply this return to the income received from the property, you can determine the property's value.

The cap rate uses three factors in figuring a property's value: income (the net operating income, or NOI), the rate of return and the value. In this formula, the elements are represented as:

I = Income
R = Rate
V = Value

Knowing any two of the three values will help you figure the third.

An investor new to apartment buildings should always know the cap rate prior to making a purchase. This will help you measure the income produced, as well as determine the maximum price you could pay for a property when you know the operating income amount.

For example, if you purchase an apartment building for $1 million and the property produces an annual NOI of $100,000, then the cap rate is 10 percent. This is because the NOI is equal to the gross rent minus property expenses.

$$\$1,000,000 \div \$100,000 = 10\%$$

If you are considering purchasing an apartment building with an NOI of $150,000 and you want to see a cap rate of 11 percent, you can compute the maximum purchase price by calculating the following:

$$\$150,000 \div 11\% = \$1,363,636 \text{ maximum purchase price}$$

Using the cap rate formula, you can see that the higher the cap rate, the lower the indicated property value. Likewise, the lower the cap rate, the higher the value. Keep in mind, however, that the cap rate assumes that you are purchasing the property using all cash. This rate does not factor in any financing terms that could affect your rate of return. I use the following as a tool when I'm teaching: The trick with cap rates is to remember when values are up, cap rates are down; and when cap rates are down, values are up. When all else fails, just look at cap rates as a percentage return on the deal.

Factors Affecting Capitalization Rates

A number of factors affect cap rates, including:

- Supply and demand
- Potential appreciation
- Tax benefits
- Cash-out potential
- Ease of financing
- Risk involved

There also are some basic guidelines that lenders and appraisers expect when valuing a complex in relation to the gross operating income (GOI):

- Vacancy factor: 5 percent of GOI
- Total operating expenses: 45-60 percent of GOI, before debt service
- Replacement reserves: 3 percent of GOI
- Repairs and maintenance: 10-20 percent of GOI
- Management: about 5 percent of GOI

Measuring the Performance of Your Investment

There are essentially three sources that will produce returns for your apartment building investment: your cash, the cash that you borrow and the cash generated by the property itself (rental income and the appreciated value of the building over time).

If you are looking to maximize your returns, you will need to measure the property's performance in terms of these three factors. In addition, if you finance part of the property, your lender will analyze your present financial condition, as well as the property's performance relative to norms in the industry and various other performance measures.

Before beginning the analysis, look for the seller's motivation to sell. Too often, I find myself telling the seller that I'm not the right buyer because they are asking more than the property is worth. I like a discount.

Financial analysts use the following fundamental ratios to measure performance:

Cap Rate versus Interest Rates Spreads

A powerful method that I discovered long ago, and that has made multimillions for many, is how these two numbers work together. Cap rate is a fancy name for a return on money, just like an interest rate is a return on money. The idea is that if you can buy a piece of commercial real estate with an 8 cap rate and borrow money at 4 percent, then the spread would be 4 points. To make this clearer: If you bought a $10 million piece of real estate with an 8 cap rate, the return would be $800,000 and the borrowed money would cost roughly $400,000 a year. That would be a difference of 4 points, or $400,000. This formula becomes more interesting as cap rates compress (go down) and interest rates go down. As long as there is a decent spread between the numbers, a healthy return can be made in a strong market.

Debt Service Coverage Ratios

Basically, the debt service coverage ratio (DSCR) is how much is left over for the bank if they end up taking the property back (the NOI/debt service). This example is based off of $1, where the first $1 of revenue goes to the bank to service the debt.

Negative cash flow: If the DSCR is less than 1, you are "underwater:"

$100,000 NOI ÷ 110,000 debt service = .91 DSCR (breaking even)

$100,000 NOI ÷ $100,000 debt service = 1.0 DSCR (positive cash flow)

$127,000 NOI ÷ $100,000 debt service = 1.27 DSCR (strong positive cash flow)

$137,000 NOI ÷ $100,000 debt service = 1.57 DSCR (stronger positive cash flow)

Another indicator that I like to look at is price per unit. For example:

Price per unit = $3,000,000 for 300 units

$3,000,000 ÷ 300 = $10,000 per unit

Expenses per unit vary from class to location, but are always valuable to understand. Another example:

Total annual operating expenses = $600,000 on 100 units

$600,000 ÷ 100 = $6,000 per unit, per year = $500 per month for 100 units

Another thing to consider is the operating expenses ratio. Apartments should be running between 40 to 60 percent in expenses. To accommodate, you can add $1,000 to $1,800 per year for all bills paid ($100 to $150 a month), metered and sub-metered.

Important Formulas

- Cash-on-cash return (CCR): cash flow before taxes and initial investment
- Income per unit (IPU): NOI per number of units

- Expense per unit (EPU): total operating expense per number of units
- Loan-to-value ratio (LTV): mortgage amount divided by appraised property value

Another valuable aspect to consider is forced appreciation. You need to know how you are going to increase the value of the apartment building, as apartment buildings are valued by their net operating income. You can increase the appreciation when you lower costs and expenses, thereby increasing income and revenue.

This is one of the reasons why I love real estate over many other investment choices. We can physically fix things and improve the assets. We can put in a park for the children; we can put in new air conditioners for families. We can paint and clean up the neighborhood. We can put in granite countertops and throw away outdated ones. We can change out the floors and build dog parks. You name it! As long as you can justify the improvements by collecting more income, the sky is the limit. The more income you collect and the less you pay out on expenses, the more valuable your asset. It's that basic.

Flipping, Payback and When to Walk Away

I learned this one the hard way. In the past, if I couldn't afford the deal, I would pass it up. But I learned that if I created a buyer's list, I could flip properties fast. So, if you can't manage the deal, think about flipping property for profit. Evaluate the cash flow. Evaluate the appreciation. Evaluate the potential equity gain. Create a buyer's list of some of your investors who have the cash to invest with you and also are looking for their own deals.

Remember: Get the apartment building under contract with assignability clauses that release your liability and can be sold to another person or entity. Negotiate your fee up front with the buyer.

Gross Potential Income versus Gross Income

At this point, it's also relevant to point out the difference between gross potential income and gross income. Gross potential income is your income in a perfect world. Gross income is your actual income in the real world.

For example, I have a 34-unit building. Its gross potential rent is $18,000 per month in collections. But there are some vacancies, and a few units have been given away with concessions, move-in specials and bonuses, so I collect only $16,000 in rent in the less-than-perfect, real world. This $16,000 is my gross income.

In short, gross potential is the potential when everything is running at 100 percent (in this case $18,000), whereas gross income is the actual collection ($16,000). Even though I collected $16,000 this month, I'm still not a hero, since I left $2,000 on the table. If you know what the gross potential is, you know how you're really doing.

Payback Period and the Rule of 72

Although the actual payback period does not take into account the riskiness of an investment or the time value of money, it is still a good initial screening tool for potential investments, as well as a guide to structure.

The Rule of 72 is used to calculate the number of years it takes to double invested money. It can also be used to calculate the cash needed to return your capital within a specific period. This rule helps investors determine what cash return they will have to achieve to get back to their original investment amount within a certain number of years.

The Rule of 72 works by dividing the number 72 by the number of years specified. As an example, if an investor wished to receive their original amount of capital back in three years, the calculation would be as follows:

$$72 \div 3 = 24$$

This tells the investor that if they want to receive their original amount of capital back in three years, they would need to achieve at least a 24 percent return.

The Rule of 72 also can be used to determine the amount of time required to pay back the investment. In order to calculate how long it will take to double your investment capital from a particular rate of return, you would divide the number 72 by the amount of the return. For example, if an investor was getting a 15 percent annual return, the investment would double in approximately five years using the calculation as follows:

$$72 \div 15\% = 4.8$$

By using the Rule of 72, investors can get a quick and accurate analysis of the deal in terms of their original capital payback, as well as how long it would take to double up based on a certain return.

This is one of my favorite ratios. If you know what your dreams cost, all you have to do is use this rule to figure out how to cash flow your dreams. This is exactly what I used before buying my dream home. I used one apartment building to pay for it!

The truth is, cash flow, not money, relieves anxiety.

When to Walk Away

Let's say you have completed your entire due diligence and gone through your "best case," "worst case" and "most likely case" scenarios. If the numbers still don't make sense, you will have an important decision to make: whether or not to make an offer. The typical real estate sales contract states that after an offer has been made and at the end of the formal inspection period, the buyer must accept the property and allow the earnest money deposit to go at risk. Otherwise, the potential buyer can opt to not accept the property and have their earnest money returned to them in full.

Your inspection may reveal conditions that differ from what the seller has represented. Some of them might make the property undesirable as a potentially profitable investment. If unacceptable conditions exist, but you still would like to go through with the purchase, you could opt to request an adjustment in the price or terms of the sale. This is certainly subject to negotiation between you and the seller. These could be the most sensitive and volatile negotiations that you encounter in the process.

What constitutes a good reason to reject the property and end the deal will vary with each investor. Most tend to draw the line at material misrepresentations by the seller. These investors believe that a seller who lies about one aspect of the property, its income or condition, is likely to have lied about many others, as well.

In reality, while occasional, minor trickery is part of the negotiation game, major misrepresentations simply are unallowable. It could be better to walk away from the property than to proceed without any idea of what additional surprises might await.

The 3 Stages of Investment

What type of investor are you? Investors typically go through three stages during their wealth-building quest: getting started, getting rich, and last—but certainly not least—staying wealthy.

Stage 1: Getting Started

Make "growth thinking" a natural part of your everyday business philosophy.

If you are a first-time investor, you are likely to be wary of entering an arena that you are unfamiliar with—especially one with a potentially expensive learning curve. But you should recognize that this arena is 90 percent psychology and 10 percent mechanics. New investors are well advised to use leverage very cautiously and not take on more debt than they are comfortable with, at least initially.

It is also a good idea to be at least somewhat involved in the management of the property to learn the ropes firsthand. This allows you to gain experience, become educated and develop personal preferences for the property type that you would most like to invest in, including the ideal style of building operation that you will use in your investment properties.

At this stage of the process, a high-risk investment in a development project or a turnaround property (such as a class D) would not be the ideal place for you to begin. Many first-time investors think that they need to buy in these areas because of the cheap price. While it's true that you could make a higher return, you must be prepared to work harder. The risk of loss is quite high in this area, even for experienced investors, and the risk increases for those with less experience.

This moment in the investment process is much better suited for newer investors to build a solid foundation for growth. A better investment for you to begin with would be more of an average-grade property that can serve as a learning platform for you to get an idea of what will be required as you move forward. This is known as a "farm play."

Stage 2: Getting Rich

After you have a few property transactions under your belt and are comfortable with the methods of investing in your chosen property type and operation, your focus very likely will turn to the maximization of your investment profits by working with either more, or larger, investments.

This second stage is considered the "get rich" phase of your investment cycle. It's where you have gained enough experience and know-how to invest in more demanding projects, which in turn will yield more return to you.

It is also at this stage where you are much better equipped to take on development or turnaround projects, because you are much more prepared and have the knowledge to step through these much more easily than you would in Stage 1. This exemplifies what is known as a "treasure chest play."

In stage two, the more challenging projects typically are much more attractive to you because of their much higher profit potential. This means you will be more comfortable with handling the risk/return curve knowing that your experience and know-how can reduce your exposure to actual risk. There is great opportunity here for massive, passive income!

In many cases, you will hear stories about investors who make huge returns, take on these challenges with experience and vigor, and make good decisions based on the knowledge gained through their experience with other property investments along the way. At this stage, real initial returns of 30 or 40 percent are not out of the question. Better yet, 100 percent or more in total returns is not only possible, but also quite likely in many cases. It's home run time!

Stage 3: Staying Wealthy

So, let's say you took on high-return—yet tedious—projects throughout stage two. Once you've reached stage three, at some point you will experience the natural tendency to slow down, enjoy the fruits of your labor, and preserve the gains realized from your investments.

At this point, turnaround and development projects are not likely to be as appealing as they once were. This is due primarily to the effort that these projects require, as well as their higher risk potential.

In stage three, you will have many options, and you likely will be able to dictate the terms under which you participate in any investment deal. In many cases, stage three investors use their knowledge and capital to structure more average investment deals that will produce above-average returns, but that won't require the effort of the more intensive, stage-two type investments.

As you move through the investment stages, you likely will find that as the size and quality of the deals increase, the average returns usually decrease. It is much easier to earn a higher percentage return on a smaller deal, but the actual dollar amount also will tend to be smaller.

This is due primarily to the competitive effects of placing large amounts of capital, and also is closely related to the presence of the numerous stage three investors who are in the "stay rich" phase. The bottom line here is that the more money available to invest, the fewer choices there are for earning an above-market rate of return.

Profit & Loss Statements, Balance Sheets and Budget Reports

It is important to understand the concept of profit and loss statement in the context of real estate. Profit and loss statement is regarded as one of the vital financial statements used by business owners, financial accountants and in real estate management for identifying profit or loss of the company during a specified time period. The profit and loss statement can also be referred as the income statement. The income statement covers the idea of profit and loss of the company within the time period of time specified in its heading. The time period of the income statement is chosen by the business or the company as it varies between businesses depending on the chosen time the business wants to prepare the income statement. Note that profit and loss statement identifies the expenses, revenues, losses and gains of a company rather than cash disbursement and cash receipt. The ability of the property manager to prepare an appropriate profit and loss account will help them to know the financial position the company. The property manager represents the owner of the property as well preserving the worth of the property through generating income. Property owners pay more attention in the profit and loss statement of the company because it shows whether the company is liquidating and propelling forward. The profit and loss statement goes a long way in helping property managers to make use of the limited resources available. A competent property manager can add value to investment by increasing the net income of the company. The reverse is true for a bad property management company. It can very damaging to the owners and asset The net income shows the willing of the property manager to invest funds in real estate in a successful manager.

The methodology of the profit and loss statement or the income statement varies among companies depending on the intricate nature of the business operation. The following can be seen in the profit and loss statement in real estate or property investing.

1. Revenues from primary and secondary activities of the company. The gross rent from the sales or rent of houses or long term assets.
2. Expenses from primary and secondary activities, including the loss on sales or rent of houses or long term assets.

However, if the total revenues on real estate and gains are subtracted from the expenses and losses on real estate, it tends to be positive or negative. When it is positive, the bottom line of the income statement is stated as the net income or net profit. But when the bottom line of the income statement is negative, it indicates that there is a net loss. To get the net income, the total revenue is subtracted from the total expenses.. Net income is needed for calculating the ending equity balance also known as balance sheet. This is why the balance sheet must be prepared after the profit and loss statement.

A financial statement cannot be complete without the balance sheet. A balance sheet is a key sources of data in analyzing investment values in real estate assets. The balance sheet is a snap shot in time of the financial balance of a company or other organization. The balance sheet shows the healthy financial position for any real estate company. The property owner knows the success of a company through the balance sheet. The property manager prepares a documented report of the company's assets and obligations, including the residual ownership claims against owner's equity at a period of time. The documented report is known as the balance sheet. A balance sheet is very vital in real estate or property investing because it helps the owners of a property or investors in real estate to know the company's net worth in a specific time. Through a well appropriate balance sheet, the property owner or the property manager would be able to know whether the company has less or more value. The balance sheet identifies if the working capital is higher or lower and if the debts are higher or lower. By the process of analyzing the balance sheet, potential investors or property managers would be able to access the capacity of the company and how they can be able to meet maturing obligations as they come due. The balance sheet as well shows the combination of liabilities and assets, the layout of equity and debt financing and the amount of return of labor or service the company have had to absorb. Hence, the balance sheet is used by external parties both financial institutions like mortgage banks and investors to examine the company's financial position before giving out loans to the company.

The balance sheet shows the financial condition of the company at a given period of time. The balance sheet explains the difference between assets on one side and liabilities and owners equity on the other side. The universal accounting principle stated that a balance sheet must the balanced. That is assets equal liabilities plus capital. ASSETS= LIABILITIES+CAPITAL OR OWNERS EQUITY.

One of the fundamental things to know about balance sheet is that the assets and liabilities must always balance. In real estate or property investing company, if the assets increase from one time period to the other, the liabilities and the capital will also increase at the same amount.

Budget report can be defined as an internal documented report used by the property manager in real estate to compare the approximated budget with the current business operation number achieved during each accounting year. The budget report was established to describe how close the budgeted expenditure was to the actual expenditure during each accounting year. It is fundamental that real estate or property investing company must have a budget report because it helps to forecast the performance of the company. Perhaps sometimes budgets are regarded as the estimated financial goals set by the company. Sometimes they can be inaccurate and can differ from the actual performance of the business. In the accounting period, the property manager estimates the budgeted amount prepared at the beginning of the accounting year to the actual amount that is been absorbed.

In real estate management or property investing company, the property managers solve problems in the business through evaluating how real and correct their predictions were. If their predictions are relatively off, they can adjust their budget appropriately.

The variance describes how close the budgeted performance is to the actual performance. The budget report follows the same format with income statement or the profit and loss account. The sales revenues are listed first followed by the operating expenses and the net operating income. When the property manager estimates the actual number to be better than the budgeted number, there is favorable variance. If your property management delivers a budget that is acceptable, accurate and inline overtime. You have winner. If your property management company is slow in getting you a budget and when they do and fail to stay true to it. It's probably a good time to get a new management company in place.

CHAPTER 5

NO MONEY DOWN FUNDING STRATEGIES

As you continue through your real estate investment career and education, you will find that acquiring apartment buildings requires at least some amount of cash from the buyer. There are times when no- or low-money-down deals are possible, but these typically are made by highly experienced investors who have reached a certain level.

It would be a good idea to prepare your personal financials for the lender. Being prepared is very important. The most common paperwork needed will be a personal financial statement and a schedule of real estate owned. They will also ask you to sign an authorization for a credit check. They will want your two most recent tax returns. Have your biography or résumé ready, too. This would be a good time to create a pro forma or business plan on the property for which you're trying to borrow money.

Take, for example, an apartment complex with 160 units that sold for $5.6 million in 2006. The U.S. Department of Housing and Urban Development (HUD) guaranteed that amount to the bank that lent the money. HUD also ended up owning the complex again, but this time, they had to sell it to my group for $3 million. (This was such a good find that I had two local banks competing for my business.)

Qualifying for the Loan

Lenders seem more interested in your liquid assets, credit score, prior real estate experience, and past and current business skills. Use whatever you can to present yourself in the best possible light in these areas. This is not a good time to be modest. You need to highlight all the areas your banker will go into at the committee meeting.

Of course, they also will evaluate the apartment building as they decide whether or not they want to own it should you default on the loan. Here, they are looking at the asset quality, sub market, operating history, current rent rolls and debt service coverage ratios.

An extremely important step at this stage in the process is generating sufficient cash and credit to close your deals. There are a variety of ways to do this.

The most important factors in buying an apartment building are the financial numbers and makeup of the property. Therefore, it is extremely important to come up with an offering price that makes sense for getting the return you need to make the property profitable. If you are unable to get the apartment building for a price that makes financial sense, then you should not even waste your time inspecting the property or going any further in the process.

Some Ideas for Financing Your Acquisitions

Strategies for funding include the following:

- Traditional financing
- Rebates
- Private money
- Seller financing
- Substitution of collateral
- Master lease option
- Creative financing
- Partnerships

Advantages of Limited Partnerships

- Fast way to raise real estate capital
- Lets you keep control of the apartment complex
- Easy legal requirements
- Few operating problems

In other words, borrow your way to a real estate fortune. Real estate is a borrowed money business. The sooner you understand this, the faster you will be wealthy!

I was able to buy larger complexes using a method I call the "Balance Sheet Net Worth." It works like this:

- Start small with a no-money-down deal
- Improve all the numbers
- Raise your rents, increase your income and decrease expenses
- Get a new appraisal
- Show your financial statement to your banks with new numbers

Typically, when people think about buying real estate, they think only of the traditional process of going to the bank and asking (or begging) for a loan. In most situations, the bank will ask for a down payment of 20 to 30 percent of the property's purchase price.

They will also need stacks of information regarding your income, credit history and just about any other piece of information they can think of. In addition, you generally cannot close on a bank-funded real estate transaction for at least 30 days—and often, even longer.

Keep in mind, however, that there are numerous other potential sources of property funding. Some may be right in front of you, while others might require you to dig a little. In any case, the more creative you can be with finding the money to fund your property, the better off you will be.

Line of Credit

A personal or business line of credit is another source of available cash. If you own a home or other property with a great deal of equity, you might find that you can borrow from a line of credit secured by the property for less than you would be able to borrow from a lender on a property mortgage.

Lines of credit are somewhat more difficult to get today than they were in the past. Still, they could be a potential source of funds. For example, if the bank charges you 5 percent for the line of credit, but your property is returning 12 percent to you, you will essentially keep the spread. The same holds true for a business line of credit. This is especially true if you are running your real estate investing as a business, such as a Limited Liability Company or another type of corporate structure.

IRA's and Retirement Accounts

Most people don't know that individuals are allowed to purchase real estate with funds held in an IRA and certain other types of retirement accounts. While many people think that IRA's and 401(k) accounts can only include basic or "traditional" investments (such as stocks, bonds and mutual funds), this is a misconception.

Most IRA and 401(k) accounts are managed by traditional brokerage and financial firms. As a result, investors are taught to think that they may invest only in these types of assets because they are the only products these types of institutions can sell.

In reality, though, investors are allowed to invest in just about any type of asset—with very few exceptions from the IRS—if they have what is known as a self-directed IRA or 401(k) retirement account.

Self-directed IRA's allow the account holder to make investment choices and investments on behalf of the retirement plan. In its basic structure and tax-advantaged status, a self-directed IRA technically is no different than other IRA accounts. However, it is unique in certain ways because of the elements of control and the large variety of available options it offers to investors.

In a self-directed IRA, the account owner directs the investments rather than being restricted only to what a broker or bank representative offers to them. By allowing a much wider range of investment choices, self-directed IRA's can improve the account holder's opportunities to diversify their portfolio into nearly limitless investment vehicles.

Along with tax-free profits and the potential for faster growth, a self-directed IRA can provide the account owner large tax deductions, asset protection features and even potential estate planning benefits.

Self-directed 401(k) plans work in a similar fashion, as long as the plan of the entire group is self-directed. In other words, if a company has a self-directed 401(k) as their retirement plan, the entire group of employees involved in the plan can invest in assets such as real estate and other assets that are considered nontraditional to the typical 401(k) plan.

Specific IRS rules accompany this procedure. As long as you have funds in the property type of self-directed retirement account, you are allowed to use those funds to buy various types of rental and other investment properties. The good news is that the rental income and capital gains from the property can flow back into those retirement accounts either on a tax-deferred or tax-free basis.

Investment Partners

A very effective strategy for buying property is teaming up with investment partners. You may find another real estate investor who is also in the process of locating property, but who needs additional funding to get the project financed. Working together and pooling your funds could yield a win-win situation on both sides.

Seller Financing

Another common source for financing real estate projects is seller financing. There are many advantages to using seller financing. Typically, there are no points or fees, no property appraisal is necessary, and there is no need to educate the lender about the property. In addition, this type of financing can offer very flexible terms.

The most common scenario is to have the seller hold a second mortgage to fill the gaps between the purchase price, your down payment amount and any first mortgage being placed by a lender or being assumed by you as the buyer.

Seller financing can be short-term or long-term, interest-only or amortizing, and with or without a balloon/call. In some cases, the seller-held note may be sold in the private market, generating cash at closing for the seller.

Mortgage Brokers and Mortgage Bankers

Mortgage brokers and mortgage bankers are another good source of funding for your apartment building purchases. Some mortgage brokerage companies and mortgage banks also can service some or all of the loans they originate.

Loan servicing includes the collection of payments, maintenance of escrow accounts (including disbursements), and servicing the lender's agent for the purpose of notice and reporting requirements. A good broker will look for conventional lending from banks, insurance companies, and Freddie Mac or Wall Street sources (such as Commercial Backed Securities, or CMBS).

Hard Money Lenders

Hard money lenders are a very popular source of short-term funds. These are individuals or institutions that offer loans with low credit restrictions in return for higher interest rates and fees. They are often considered lenders of last resort for those who may need a loan under unique conditions.

In most cases, hard money lenders are private investors—individuals who use hard money loans to increase their wealth through the high interest rates charged on the loans they provide.

Most hard money loans are for the purpose of funding real estate purchases. In nearly every case, the property itself is used as the loan collateral. Because these types of loans are quite risky for the lender, most hard money lenders will personally inspect the property prior to lending any money to see what they are funding in the case of borrower default.

As previously discussed, to secure a traditional real estate loan from a bank, you typically need good credit, income and references. However, none of this is necessary in the case of a hard money loan. Hard money lenders deal with loans that most traditional financial lenders refuse. Therefore, they look less at a borrower's credit and more at the potential return on the investment itself. Since most hard money lenders are individual investors, they are less common than ordinary banks and lenders.

Interest rates and fees on hard money loans usually are significantly higher than traditional loan rates, although there is no single, typical hard money loan rate. In many cases, a borrower should expect to pay double or even triple the interest that a traditional lender would charge.

Hard money loans primarily are used in quick turnaround situations, for short-term financing needs, and/or by borrowers who have poor credit but a substantial amount of equity in their property.

Commercial, National and Regional Banks

Commercial banks provide some services similar to those of a traditional bank, such as accepting deposits and providing business loans. However, they offer many different services, as well. These include underwriting, acting as an intermediary between an issuer of securities and investors, facilitating mergers and other types of corporate reorganizations, and acting as a broker for their institutional clients.

National mega banks have brand names, multi-billions of dollars in assets and committees that run the organization. It is rare for one, single person to have any significant approval power, which is why committees are designed to make sure that nothing out of the ordinary takes place. It is often difficult to obtain financing from these types of banks.

Regional banks may hold anywhere from one billion to many billions of dollars in assets. These banks typically have a consumer focus. They may have several branches across a particular state or region, and they usually target the retail customer in their advertising. These banks are also a good source for construction, rehab and bridge loans.

People today are caught up in the hype that banks aren't lending. A lot of banks experienced significant, hard hits with losses to their portfolio. They're setting aside capital to deal with it and not doing a lot of lending. With regard to apartment loans, however, banks—especially local banks—are lending. In fact, the situation has never been better! Maybe the big banks are still putting out all the fires they started, but the little guys are sliding in there under the radar to refinance their neighborhoods. There's no better way for a bank to be in business than to lend to people in their local area for applied housing.

Warren Buffet once said that his organization was in the business of buying dollars for 50 cents. It could happen that you walk into a bank and show them that you're proposing to buy a dollar for 50 cents, and they still don't want to lend you money. In that case . . . well, just leave. That particular bank is not lending that week. Find one that is lending.

Maybe 63 banks have been closed down this year, but there are still thousands and thousands of banks out there.

Be the one in the few who walks into a bank, head held high, with the information in this book. Show them a deal they can't refuse. Show them a deal that cash flows from day one and has millions of dollars in equity in case they were ever to take it back. After all, banks have to lend to stay in business.

Conduit Loans

Conduit loan is a catch-all term for a host of different lenders that are in some way connected to the securities markets. The fundamentals of the business rely on bundling a number of similar loans for sale as CMBS. This source of lending is becoming very popular again. It's short-term lending that fills the gaps of bridging long-term debt. It's like working with a hard money lender, but at cheaper rates and with fewer requirements.

Insurance Companies

Life insurance companies are a fantastic source of financing. In fact, they financed two of my three most recent deals. Insurance companies are still active players in the commercial real estate mortgage market. They typically have large sums of money available and can generally offer low-cost funds. In addition, they've got to take care of their holders and pay out at 6 to 8 percent per month to annuities. We've been living in a 0 to 1 percent world. Not everyone can simply hold onto money; they have to reinvest it, so they're aggressively lending money to people who want to buy apartment buildings.

Some conduit and insurance company loans are said to be "non-recourse." This means that the lender will look to the property itself for repayment of the loan, and not to the personal assets of the borrower.

However, there are certain items that are always exempt from the non-recourse provision. These are known as carve-outs, and they typically include environmental liability issues and any fraudulent act on the part of the borrower in seeking the loan or subsequent to the closing.

These clauses have become so standard that they generally are referred to as "the usual carve-outs for environmental and fraud."

Conventional Loans

Conventional loans are mortgages that are not insured or guaranteed by any government agency, including the Federal Housing Administration (FHA), Farmers Home Administration (FMHA) and Department of Veterans Affairs (VA).

These loans generally have fixed rates and terms. They abide by the guidelines set by Fannie Mae (the Federal National Mortgage Association), a corporation created by the federal government to buy and sell conventional mortgages. It sets the maximum loan amount and the requirements for borrowers.

In many cases, conventional loans are for 30-year, fixed-rate mortgages. These loans have fixed interest rates for the entire 30-year term of the loan, and generally require at least a 20 percent down payment.

As an example, if an apartment building is to be purchased for $500,000, you would need a down payment amount of $100,000. The conventional loan would finance the other $400,000.

Typically, conventional loans have a better interest rate than non-conventional loans, and they can be a great option for real estate purchasers who have 20 percent of the purchase price to put down on the property. If you do not have 20 percent to put down, there is still a way to obtain a conventional loan. This could mean accepting a higher interest rate or adhering to other terms in return for a higher percentage of the funding needed.

Private Lenders

Similar to partners, private lenders want to make a substantial return on their money. In its most basic form, a private lender could be a friend or family member who loans you some funds for your real estate deals. They also could be an experienced lender used to loaning hundreds of thousands of dollars to real estate investors on a much larger scale.

Borrowing money from private sources can be a great way to fund your apartment building transactions. In most instances, the lender is primarily interested in the profit potential of the property itself and not in your personal credit, income or other debts. Because of this, your transactions can be processed much more quickly, allowing you to receive the funds you need right away. This often means the difference between getting a deal and not getting a deal. A seller might even accept a lower offer on their property because a buyer has cash in hand and can close quickly.

There really are no rules for private lending. Essentially, you get what you negotiate because there aren't any guidelines. Over time, however, you will notice some patterns that you can rely on. For example, you should try to obtain the lowest possible interest rate at the lowest possible cost. So, when you begin speaking with potential private lenders, you should first map out what you are willing to accept and deal with at the outset.

For instance, get an idea of the worst-case scenario that you would settle for and stick to it. You should approach private lending situations in the same way that you would with making an offer on the property itself. Conversely, you should also have a best-case scenario in mind before you begin negotiating with the lender. (Of course, the private lender will also have an idea of what is acceptable.)

There are a number of places where you can find private lenders. Some include:

- Business organizations
- Seminars
- Real Estate Investment Association (REIA) groups
- Real estate agents/brokers
- Create partnerships

There are also a number of creative financing ideas you can take advantage of to borrow private money, such as:

- Seller carry back
- Private equity partnerships

- Cross collateralization
- Blanket funding
- Private notes

Some investors develop an extensive list of potential private lenders that they can call upon depending on the particular deal they are working on. In order to truly be successful in finding the funds you need, you must get over your fear of asking people for money.

When you begin to close deals with private lenders, you should have some standard terms. Although most hard money lenders typically will tell you what terms they offer, when you are working with private lenders, you are the one who dictates the terms of the deal.

Although all of the loan's terms may be negotiable, it is much better for you to set the terms up front. This is proactive for your future investments, as it would be nearly impossible to have different terms for every single, private lender with whom you work. Besides putting you in greater control of the deal, having standardized terms makes things much easier to manage—especially if you start to do multiple transactions simultaneously.

Some of the terms that you will need in your deals with private lenders are discussed below.

Points (Funding Fees)

Points are also referred to as "origination fees" or "discount fees." They are essentially interest that is paid up front. You can pay your private lenders points as a fee to do the deal. With longer-term deals, you might not need to pay points. You still could offer them to help sweeten the deal for the lender.

Also, if the deal needs to be funded quickly, you might need to offer a point (or points) to the lender in return for obtaining your funds quickly. Typical hard money lenders may charge 5 or more points, but you will likely not need to pay your hard money lenders this much. You should have standard terms regarding points that you pay your private lenders, such as 1.5 points per deal.

Length of Loan

The length of time during which you borrow money from private lenders most will often be determined by the particular deal. Some loans could be as short as six months, while others could be as long as several years.

Payment Schedule

Payment schedule refers to how and when you will pay interest to your private lenders. You can be more flexible on your payment schedule. In many cases, the payment schedule depends on the lender's needs or habits. For example, you could offer monthly or quarterly interest payments, or you could offer to pay out all proceeds at the end of the deal.

Loan-To-Value (Purchase Price versus After-Repair Value)

In a case where a property is being rehabbed, the fee structure should match the loan-to-value, or LTV. If at all possible, you should not go any higher than that amount.

Rehab Work

Again, the variable refers to the fact that some private lenders will fund only the property, while others will fund both the property and any needed rehab work.

Tax and Insurance Escrows

You must remember to pay taxes and insurance on your property. These are not included in the regular payment schedule because private lenders don't escrow for taxes and insurance.

Equity Split

A private lender sometimes will want to be your partner in the deal. With this option, the lender can receive a percentage of the profit on the deal.

Although this option may sound good up front, it is a fairly expensive way for you to get your deal funded. Hold on to the equity if you can.

Capital Stack

It is truly possible to build an empire by leveraging yourself through others! Mixing and matching these strategies will help you fund your deals. One potential combination might be to use private money for the down payment and a CMBS loan to close the deal. Then, three to five years later, refinance into a 25- to 30-year loan (also known as your "capital stack").

Here is an example of capital stack:

First Stack	5% private money
Second Stack	15% bridge lender or a mezzanine loan
Third Stack	80% CMBS Loan
Fourth Stack	New conventional loan; all of the first three levels have been paid back!

Good questions to ask about the borrowed money include the following:

- What is the amount of the loan?
- What is the interest rate?
- What are the repayment terms?
- What is the yield spread?
- Are there prepayment penalties?
- What are the funding fees?

Developing Relationships with Banks and Private Lenders
Banks

People who earn a living by working with money are intimidating to many investors. Banks are in the business of selling other people's money for profit, and real estate investors are in the business of using other people's money to make a profit. But think: This is actually a win-win situation! By working together, each can obtain their objective. The trick is to balance each entity's respective interests.

When you approach a bank in need of a loan, you likely will get the standard response of needing 25 percent cash down, a personal guarantee and a long-term amortization on the loan.

The introductory call from a local professional will help the banker learn a little more about you and your real estate business, while also helping to establish a common interest before you even meet. Assuming that the conversation goes well and the banker likes the sound of the deal, they will either agree to take a look at the deal or refer you to a subordinate responsible for working on commercial real estate deals.

Since your meeting originated from the people at the top, this likely will create a major shift in perception for the person with whom you will be working in processing your loan. The loan officer will know immediately that you are someone that the bank's senior management has an interest in working with. They will either take your call immediately or perhaps even initiate a call to you! Also, because this loan officer has been given advance notice of what you are going to be discussing, they will surely be current on the bank's loan products available to fit your specific funding situation.

When you initially meet in person with the bank's loan officer or senior manager, the immediate goal is simply to get acquainted. You should take a copy of your company's portfolio, as well as a brief written history of your company and your real estate investing history. In addition, you should include information on the background of your company's principals as well as photos of your real estate holdings.

When speaking with the bank representative, you will want to get answers to some basic questions regarding the bank's lending policies and criteria. This might include information about rates, loan-to-value ratios and debt coverage requirements.

Private Lenders

You also could advertise proactively for private lenders. This will bring lenders to you, rather than making you have to go directly to them. You will often see ads on various websites and local and national newspapers from people seeking funding. These ads will draw the attention of potential private lenders, as there are always investors looking for places to put their money, regardless of the state of the economy. Place your newspaper ad in sections such as "Joint Ventures" or "Money to Invest." This is an easy place to start.

The scope and profitability of your project will dictate where you should advertise. Of course, the larger the property and profit potential, the more you can afford to spend, and the more websites and/or newspapers you can afford to advertise in.

There also might be times when you get responses from your ads after a project has been funded. Do not turn away these individuals! You should invite them to be placed on your mailing list to be contacted for future projects. This way, you are continually collecting a bank of leads from people who already are interested in funding your deals. This will save you a great amount of time and money in the long run, as eventually you will have a contact list of potential private lenders that can be emailed or called instantly as you move on to your future projects.

Get Your Pitch Ready!

It's time for you to tell your story. The single most successful way I have found to raise money is through private individuals. Around 70 to 80 percent of the money needed to purchase a complex will come from a bank. You're almost there! You just need to raise around 20 to 30 percent of the purchase price. Public speaking and sharing your story in two minutes can mean the difference between working for others or an eight-digit financial net worth: financial freedom!

Here is a sample script you could use to pitch your project to private lenders:

> *"Do you have an IRA or any other investment capital that's not getting you a 15 percent return safely? I buy, sell and hold multifamily apartment buildings, and sometimes borrow short-term funds from individuals such as you to purchase and redevelop these apartment buildings. I currently own over 100 single-family houses, 1,000 apartment units, and run and self manage a $25 million real estate portfolio.*
>
> *"I have worked with many people just like you. I'm a value buyer. For the last few years, I have been buying apartment buildings, bank*

foreclosures, government foreclosures, deals at auctions and deals in receivership being liquidated by judges. We purchase these apartment buildings at less than half their market value. Sometimes we fix them, fill them up or just operate them as is. This gives me a huge advantage over my competition. It allows me to decide if I want to buy, sell or hold. I can offer the best product, best price and best value to my investors and tenants.

"Your money is secured by a mortgage. I pay__ % interest, plus up to a few months of extra interest when I pay off your loan. All loans are closed by professionals with title insurance, fire insurance, appraisals and other proper documentation. I never borrow more than the property can support.

"Would you be interested in making a safe return of __ % on your money?"

Investing Your Time Wisely

There is a lot to say about lifestyle and the course you're on at this stage. It's important to always be improving your skills, as this will have a direct result on how you grow your real estate business. I do the following to improve:

- Watch little or no television
- Read for 30 minutes every morning
- Tell yourself that you're the best
- Read for 15 minutes a day about maintaining a positive attitude
- Read one sales book a quarter
- Read one personal development book a quarter
- Read one creativity book a year
- Attend four sales seminars a year
- Listen to podcasts twice as often as the radio while in the car
- Record yourself reading a book on sales
- Post your goals where you see them often, and recite them out loud twice a day
- Engage in real sales training for 30 minutes a week during sales meetings with your friends or co-workers
- Record yourself making a sales presentation
- Tear out this list and keep it handy

CHAPTER 6

DEAL STRUCTURE AND EXIT STRATEGIES FOR MASSIVE WEALTH

Determining the Offer Price

You must consider numerous factors when preparing to make an offer on a property. Certainly, the physical characteristics (such as location and structure) will play a part. However, to truly profit from your investment, you will also have to decipher whether there is any "upside" in the property that could increase your return.

An "upside" is a situation that can yield profits over and above the normal appreciation from improving a property's performance. Typically, to improve performance, you must either increase income, reduce expenses or both.

Value Theories

There are various methods of determining the price of an apartment building. One of the most popular methods used by commercial real estate brokers is coming up with an asking price on an income property that is equal to the market cap rate applied to the property's NOI.

The market cap rate is the median indicated cap rate of recent sales for comparable properties in a particular market area. In order for this rate to be used to determine value, the rate extracted from market data must accurately reflect two specific elements: the conditions of the sale and the NOI. This is important because brokers in a community will rely fairly heavily on this assumption.

It is also extremely important to decipher the difference between the actual selling price of a comparative property and the terms of the sale. The sales price of a property is often a matter of public record. What is not always disclosed, however, is pertinent information related to the terms of that sale.

These might include seller concessions, seller financing at below-market rates, or the grouped sale of more than one property. Without knowing this important information, the cap rate will have very little basis in the market or even to the subject property.

Net Operating Income

The exact net operating income (NOI) of any property is known only by the property owner and a few other principals involved in the property's management. In addition, even with exact numbers given, this NOI figure can result in different figures, depending on whether the numbers relate to the historical income for the past year's operation, the broker's pro forma projections for sales purposes or the projected income under the buyer's ownership.

In addition, you will need to know whether the estimated NOI reflects a replacement reserve. The selling broker likely will have access only to the offering information—usually a pro forma projection of normalized operations—and not the actual income used by a buyer to determine the price to be paid.

In many cases, each investor will estimate the NOI independently. The only true way to obtain the figures would be to get the details of the transaction from a principal in each deal. Since this information is held in the strictest confidence, this normally is not feasible.

Without access to accurate income figures and sales terms, the cap rate determined is essentially just an educated guess. Many assumptions must be drawn from lease rates and expenses to determine the NOI. Because of this, more often than not, only a "range of value" can be established.

Asking Price

Many investors simply use the seller's asking price as a starting point in determining an offer price. Yet, in reality, this approach requires a huge amount of faith in areas over which you, the buyer, have absolutely no control.

This method also can play a large part in whether or not your investment will prove to be profitable. The outcome relies more on simply "winning" the price negotiation with the seller and has very little to do with what the property is actually worth, both now and in the future.

Appraised Value

A widely accepted value determination is the property's appraised value as rendered by a competent professional property appraiser. This person typically will be active in the marketplace and will have access to the databases and research materials necessary for the market and property type.

In addition, an appraiser will have access to specific buy-side information that could help you as the buyer. The buy-side calculation begins with known factors of income based on the buyer's calculation of both net operating income and price. This also includes the conditions of the sale, and can help in solving the unknown cap rate.

Approaches to Value

When researching the appraisal of a commercial property, you will find that the appraiser typically uses three approaches to determine a property's value: the comparable sales method, the replacement cost method and the income approach.

A commercial property appraiser usually will evaluate a property using each of these approaches and will make a final determination of value based on a weighted average of the methods in a process known as reconciliation of value. This is the value that reflects the combined market factors, the property condition and terms of the sale.

Comparable Sales Method

The comparable sales method, or "comps" as it is often called, probably is the most familiar method, and is often the very best indicator for determining the value of single-family, residential real estate.

Using the comparable sales method, the property appraiser collects sales data from recent transactions within a specific radius from the subject property and adjusts the data for location, size, quality and other factors to get an accurate comparison to the subject property.

Replacement Cost Method

Imagine if your property burned down or was blown away by a hurricane. In order to come up with the property's replacement costs, it would be necessary to first deconstruct the components of that property. Then, each component must be assigned a current value and adjusted for age and condition.

In cases such as this, a property appraiser performs a build-out analysis for the property as if it were new construction. The property then is adjusted for the depreciated value of the improvements.

Income Approach

For income-generating properties, the income approach usually is given the most weight in the final reconciliation of the property's value. By definition, this method requires accurate input of the operational data for both the property itself and the corresponding market.

Structuring the Deal

In putting together your offer, you will need to structure the deal to realize profit on your own terms, in your own time frame and with a built-in margin for safety. Personally, I like to under-promise and over-deliver.

There essentially are four components to structuring a deal: the investment objective, the investment plan, the financing and your exit strategy. The relationship among all of these factors will help drive the overall profit potential of any real estate deal.

Investment Objective

The objective of your investment is your true intentions regarding what you wish to do with it. Specifically, will you hold the property or will you resell it within a short time ("flip" it)?

You might intend to acquire the property as a long-term investment (a period of three or more years), or you might decide to resell quickly. This one decision will establish the basis for all of your other investment-related decisions about the property.

A property "flip" is defined as a property purchase and sale that take place within one year. In many cases, the property is in distressed condition. This means that the owner is unable to expose the property to normal market channels, so the purchase is made at a substantial discount.

An investor in this scenario might refurbish the property and resell it through more conventional channels at price closer to a normal market price. The flipping strategy is quite often used with single-family residential properties, but the concept is very similar when used with commercial properties.

Regardless of whether you plan to hold a property for the short or long term, your decisions regarding the scope of work performed, market position and leasing strategies should be made with just one goal in mind: increasing value.

It also should be noted that even though you will decide to go in a particular direction with a property, that decision is not always carved in stone. You are free to change your intent at any time. Investors often buy a property with the plan to flip it as soon as renovations are completed, but along the way, become convinced that the property would have more value if held in their portfolio for the long term. You can always refinance your money out of the deal and cash flow the property.

Investment Plan

The investment strategy of determining whether to flip or hold a property must fit into your overall investment plan. Some investors buy just one property with the intention of focusing solely on that investment for a short or long period of time. Others, however, may own (or plan to own) numerous properties. In any case, each individual property investment will need to fit into your specific, overall investment plan.

Financing

More often than not, investors are unable to pay for their properties entirely in cash. Even investors with access to cash will still seek ways to fund their properties, in most instances. Getting a deal to go through likely will require at least some amount of financing. The type of loan used must also correspond to the nature of the overall project.

Exit Strategy

You formulate your exit strategy by breaking down your business into its core functions: strategy, marketing, innovation, management and so on. Next, allocate these functions in terms of highest importance and best use of time. Build your business on a foundation of multiple profit sources instead of depending on a single revenue stream.

Pyramiding Your Assets

The reality is that the shortest path to building real wealth in real estate is through pyramiding your assets. In other words, you should be able to retain and enhance the flow of benefits from current investments in order to increase your capital.

That capital then is used to acquire additional assets. Like the pyramids I visited in Giza, Egypt, your assets will begin to build on each other. This, however, can tend to create an interesting situation on just how you retain assets and yet use that same capital for the purpose of acquiring more. Many real estate investors become comfortable, or even complacent. Pyramiding forces us to continue to grow and buy more assets, and thus continue to build our portfolios and cash flows. Eventually, the process becomes self-fulfilling and very rewarding, and has been responsible for building generations of wealth for many investors.

Combined with some IRS codes, such as a 1030 exchange, taxes can be deferred for decades while cash flows and equity are built. This is a solution to the puzzle of net worth: Why pay taxes on gains today, if we can continue to live off the greater cash flows? If your investment objective is to sell your property once it is stabilized, that sale might be structured under Section 1031 of the IRS tax code, which, in essence, will allow the pyramiding of equity into a larger property.

Prior to any sale or property exchange, however, you might want to consider obtaining a new, assumable permanent loan that is structured as a cash-out refinance. This will generate tax-free cash, making the assumable loan and property more attractive to another investor or buyer.

It's important to correctly document all of your improvements so that you can easily hand over all necessary paperwork to the buyer during due diligence. Save all invoices, receipts and photos. Have all of your documents ready to go and be prepared to hand them over to your buyer to help facilitate the due diligence process.

CHAPTER 7
Due Diligence: Property Inspection and Rebates

The Importance of a Thorough Property Inspection

I nvesting in an apartment building is a huge financial commitment, a decision that should not be made lightly. To know exactly what you are getting into, a thorough inspection of the property is an absolute must.

Many potential problem areas in a large, commercial property simply cannot be found during a casual walkthrough. In order to uncover any potential problems before you purchase, it is necessary to delve deeper and assess such features as the foundation, the supporting structures and the roof.

One reason that an inspection is so important is that it gives you advance notice of any problems already present. Issues such as water damage, termite damage and the presence of asbestos can be revealed with a thorough inspection. Finding these issues and rectifying them before the deal is closed is essential.

An inspection report also can give you extra bargaining power when negotiating price. By pointing out any issues and the cost to repair them, you often can negotiate a lower purchase price.

In addition to a physical inspection, you also will want to inspect the financial and accounting records of the property to get a true idea of what is happening with tenants, rents and expenses.

When searching for good apartment properties to purchase, you'll want to focus on properties where current tenants are paying less rent than what you know the units could go for.

Remember: You are not just going inspect the actual condition of the property itself, but also the individual units. It's important to assess whether you could get more rent than the current owner is getting and what steps (if any) you will need to take to get top-of-the-market rent amounts.

A lot of distressed sellers and property management companies handling a bank-owned property that has been through auctions, receiverships or special servicing are just trying to keep the property stable and get it off their books. They are not interested in raising rents. Their main goal is to keep occupancy high to make the property attractive for disposition.

Once you buy the property, identify and fix all the problems, you can reintroduce yourself to tenants and make a statement to the effect of, "Look, I realize you might be upset about the way things have been going here for the last 12 months. But I'm here now. This is a big investment and I'm not going anywhere. But I'll tell you what: I have to raise the rent just like rents have been raised at the rest of the apartment buildings on the block, and I'm sorry if you feel like you have to move. But if you stay, I want you to know that I'm going to make the following changes . . ."

In just about any apartment complex, you probably will have units that need work in terms of things like paint, carpet replacement and/ or new appliances. Some complexes may have lobbies or other common areas that need also sprucing up.

Once you have inspected the units, ask yourself if you are going to be able to raise the rents of the apartments in their existing condition, and if so, by how much? Will some work be required? Is the current property owner renting the units to tenants at a discount?

Inspecting the Actual Property and Premises
A number of factors go into a commercial property inspection. It is important to choose a properly trained commercial property inspector to get the best evaluation possible.

The term "deferred maintenance" describes defects that have been overlooked and must be fixed in order to preserve the property's long-term health. These items are different from capital improvements that can ensure—as well as improve—the property's long-range income stream.

Knowing the difference between deferred maintenance and capital improvements is critical when you are evaluating a property, because you will need to account for all funds required to fix the property. When you move to the valuation stage in the decision to buy, these costs will be determined as being deducted dollar-for-dollar against the indicated valuation of the property.

Building Systems

It is particularly important when evaluating a possible real estate investment to inspect the performance as well as the condition of the infrastructure and delivery systems for the utilities, including HVAC (heat, ventilation and air conditioning) and trash removal. If you do not have any experience in testing these types of systems, you need to hire a professional to both inspect the property and deliver a report. It is important to have someone with a trained eye inspect these items. These systems might be in good working order now, but they could fail in the future.

One example is galvanized water lines. Galvanized pipe was the material of choice in the 1950's through 1980's. It was inexpensive, readily available and very adaptable to a wide variety of construction methods, including frame, block and slab.

Unfortunately, the life span of galvanized pipe is quite a bit shorter than the useful life of the actual properties they serve, lasting only about 20 years on average. It is important to know these types of things because repairing and/or replacing plumbing for an entire apartment complex should the pipe fail would come at quite a steep cost! I know many apartment owners who have had to replace their galvanized pipes 10 feet at a time when something leaks—not a fun experience.

Likewise, you must have the property's sewer lines and roof inspected as well. Take, for example, terra cotta, a clay-like material that was used for sewer lines for many years, primarily in the American Southwest. Similarly, flat composition roofs found in the southern United States are almost always in need of repair. Depending on the actual design and materials used, there are times when no permanent fix at all is feasible. Replacing these materials with rubber coating or replacing the ballast/ drains can be very costly, as well as highly disruptive to your tenants.

When viewing a building for potential purchase, you must pay very close attention to the design and condition of the roof to get an idea of how much life it has left. The cost of replacing a roof, especially on larger properties, is something that usually cannot be paid out of your normal operating revenues; you would need to have a large amount of funds set aside.

Ways to Engage in a Real Estate Transaction

There are a few options for completing the purchase. One thing you will need to keep in mind, however, is how you essentially will work with the seller to make the deal work for both parties.

In reality, all that really happens in a real estate transaction is as follows: a property's buyer and a seller of property will find a way to give the seller his or her equitable interest in the property so that they can walk away happy. I have found four primary ways to accomplish this, regardless of whether or not you have any money down. More important in the purchase of real estate is the actual concept, not the dollar amount. You can apply most concepts to any property, regardless of its price.

What you first must do, however, is define what "equity" really means. In essence, equity is the market value of a property, minus the value of any liens or encumbrances on that property. The most common encumbrance is a loan secured by the property. The loan can be referred to either as a mortgage or as a trust deed, depending on the state in which the property is located.

The loan can be either a first or second (or third, etc.) mortgage or deed of trust. Other encumbrances or liens may include unpaid property taxes, mechanics' liens or even unpaid judgments in small claims court.

Four Ways of Purchasing Real Estate
Pieces

One way to have the seller receive equitable interest in a real estate transaction is to provide it in "pieces." Think of the seller's equity in the property as being owned in pieces or payments. Should the seller receive their equity in pieces—and the bank or lender on the mortgage also continue to receive their equity in pieces—then the actual sale could take place.

Everybody who has an equitable interest in the property will then be satisfied. In this situation, pieces will go to the sellers for their equity in the property, and also to the bank or lender on the mortgage, until the equitable interest is fully transferred.

Lump Sum

Another way that a property seller can receive equity is in the form of a lump sum. In this case, the transaction could entail a cash purchase. Or, the buyer could obtain a new mortgage on the property and simply make a down payment in cash for the balance owed on the property's purchase price. This can also be referred to as a cash-to-loan transaction.

The bank or lender on the property's mortgage or deed will be paid off when the new loan is made, and the seller will subsequently receive cash for their portion of the equity in the property that has been sold.

"Different Form"

Another way that a seller could receive equity from the property being sold is under a "different form." The seller's equity can be paid with just about anything that has a perception of value that the seller considers equal to their equity in the property.

Rather than cash, the seller may agree to take another property in trade, or perhaps something else of value, such as stock. The possibilities are practically endless.

A Combination of the Three

The fourth way that a seller can receive equity for a property being sold is through a combination of these three methods: pieces, lump sum and different form. This option leads to endless combinations of ways to compensate the seller.

One way to come up with an acceptable form of payment is to first identify the seller's needs and perception of value. Once this has been accomplished, it will be much easier to put together a deal, as long as the seller considers what you have to offer to be a fair value exchange for the property.

Letter of Intent

As an interested potential buyer, you have the option to present a letter of intent (LOI) to the seller before going to an actual contract. These basically are contracts put into place before an official contract comes into being. In essence, an LOI is a letter that states that a contract will occur between the two parties, and thus can be considered a "pre-contract."

An LOI may be used to establish very specific, clear points in an otherwise complicated contract. This can be useful for putting the future contract in more easily understandable portions for the seller's agent/broker to share. It even can help the seller better understand some of the terms that might materialize with the sale.

It is important to understand that an LOI does not obligate either party to perform any act related to the sale or purchase of the property. It does, however, obligate the parties to perform the process as agreed upon in the letter.

The stated terms in an LOI can be modified to suit any situation, keeping in mind the necessity to incorporate the basic elements of price, terms and timing of the sale. The letter also can be used as a template for the actual purchase agreement.

It is customary, as well as highly advisable, for the buyer to prepare and deliver the first draft of the purchase agreement to the seller. The seller or their counsel can then respond to any areas of concern, and the parties will subsequently work out the appropriate language to accommodate their respective interests.

Typically in these cases, if the two parties are unable to agree on the basic terms before moving into the actual contract negotiations, there won't be a deal. The LOI gets the deal on solid footing before any money is exchanged, while simultaneously telling the property seller that they can supply the information requested to move forward with the deal.

Sometimes, rather than simply accepting an LOI, the seller or their broker may request an executed purchase contract prior to releasing any further due diligence materials or information, such as the property's actual operating statements or tax returns. There are times when real estate contract negotiations can drag on over the exact wording and terms of a deal.

In some cases, however, this is understandable. The seller is advised to be on the lookout for all types of situations. If a seller feels that you are going to flip the property prior to closing or perform another type of creative situation, the seller needs to know that you are a serious buyer.

There are other cases where the property's listing broker dreads the situation of other brokers being involved in "daisy chains" of two or more brokers between the listing broker and the end buyer's broker. In turn, market seller brokers are common. If you want to bring a buyer's broker into the transaction, it will cost another 3 to 5 percent.

As a legitimate buyer, your intent should be to build rapport with the seller and inform them of your intent. Once you've established a relationship, you can call for action by reiterating the terms of the LOI. In many cases, this will help the seller overcome any suspicions of "game playing." It also helps all parties involved to get on with the transaction.

CHAPTER 8

FILLING VACANCIES AND MANAGING FOR CASH FLOW

How to Properly Operate and Manage Your Properties

I ncome properties, especially larger investments such as apartment complexes, require someone to physically be present to oversee marketing and leasing, rent collection, property maintenance, financial record keeping (such as accounting and reporting procedures) and the implementation of overall decisions regarding asset management.

The people you choose to make these decisions and perform these duties will have a significant effect on your investment, from the initial valuation to the eventual sale. Your choice of property manager also will involve a lifestyle commitment from the moment you purchase the property.

Therefore, the process of finding a truly qualified and competent property manager should not be taken lightly. In fact, this will be one of your most important decisions regarding the type of investments you choose to pursue. This decision ultimately will affect your lifestyle, as well as the overall returns from the property and the ultimate soundness of your investment portfolio.

The good news is that you do not have to choose from an exceedingly long list of options. The options can be mixed and matched, providing a number of alternatives for lifestyle, ability and cost.

There are essentially five ways in which income properties can be managed:

- Managing the property yourself
- Having a resident manager, whom you supervise

- Hiring a management company to perform all property management duties
- Hiring a professional property manager
- Managing assets with property managers

Certainly, each of these methods has benefits and drawbacks.

Managing the Property Yourself

Before you decide to "save money" and manage the property yourself, you need to do a thorough and very honest self-assessment of both your available time and temperament for the required tasks. If you are employed full time and/or have a family (especially one with small children), and/or if you desire any semblance of free time, managing the property yourself may not be your best option. I have found that many new owners want to be involved when they're first starting out. I, for one, worked at my first apartment complex.

If you decide that you have the time and expertise to manage the property yourself, understand that you likely will need to be involved full-time, especially if you own a multi-unit apartment building. If you provide the management yourself, you certainly will gain the maximum return on your investment, since you will be saving a considerable fee that otherwise would go to someone else.

If you do not relish the thought of fixing broken toilets, painting walls, steam cleaning carpets or being the janitor on Saturday mornings, self-management of your property could still be an option, but with the use of subcontractors to perform any duties you do not wish to take on. If you have a limited amount of time, or if you do not consider yourself skilled in any of these areas, then hiring subcontractors for various duties can serve as a means of compensation.

Cost is another consideration. Any property management service will charge a fee; however, when you self-manage your property, remember that you are performing a tradeoff: your time for money saved. The expense of a third party management service in any form will come directly from the bottom line return on your investment. It takes a certain level of incoming revenue to afford a paid management service, and this needs to be accounted for in your initial property valuation.

Having a Resident Manager

Your first level of being an absentee owner is hiring an on-site or resident manager to take care of day-to-day operations. This person will regularly deal with tenants, and will also take care of any minor maintenance.

In many smaller apartment complexes, the resident manager might even live rent-free in return for management duties. In most instances, though, the apartment must have at least 21 units for this type of arrangement to be cost-effective.

If your resident manager is willing to accept free rent in exchange for doing the job, and your target management expense is 5 percent, you can determine whether this is cost effective with the

In most cases, these duties will include making minor repairs to apartment units, painting, picking up trash and acting as the main point of contact for tenant communications. If you go too far beyond basic duties, you might end up being disappointed.

In addition to being very clear on what the resident manager's duties will be, you must be even clearer on how much authority the resident manager will have. This authority might or might not spill over into authorizing repairs or making various agreements with tenants.

It is wise not to give your resident manager the authority to perform anything but the most minor electrical and plumbing repairs, as well as any other type of repair affecting tenant safety, unless the resident manager is specifically licensed to do such work.

Hiring Fee Management

The most common type of property management used with apartment buildings is the fee management approach. Often, local real estate companies will run side businesses offering property management services to investors in apartments and other properties. There are also companies that focus solely on this type of business.

Fees set by the property management companies typically are based on a percentage of the property's collected gross revenue. In return for that fee, the property management company will take care of leasing, collecting rent checks and providing maintenance. The company also will provide the absentee owner with a monthly accounting of all revenues and expenses from the property. This also will likely include a list of charges, such as administrative fees added to repair costs. This is something to be aware of when considering this type of property management method.

Property management companies typically manage a number of different properties. This enables them to obtain discounts from maintenance and supply chains due to the large volume of materials purchased. Some will pass along these savings to the property owner, and some will not.

You have a few options: You can do it yourself and lose sleep, hire a resident manager or hire a property management company. Property management companies shield you from all management-related hassles. You let them do their job, pay them their 3 to 5 percent of collected gross income, and spend your time looking for more deals. More importantly, you can spend your time the way you want to spend it. For me, it's being with my family.

When I started using property management services, I had more time to look at and take apart the deals that came across my desk; this exploded my wealth. And I am certain that freeing up your time will do the same for your wealth. No way am I going to volunteer to get that maintenance call at three in the morning!

Lessons Learned When Using a Bad Property Management Company

I also have experience with bad property management companies. I'd like to share some of the tricks of the trade, not to scare you away from using them, but to educate you to make well-informed decisions.

Management Kickbacks

Vendors seduce property managers and management company owners into using their services in return for discounts and gifts. From baseball tickets to cash kickbacks, I have seen it all. Unfortunately, these savings are not returned to the property owners.

Property Management Construction Companies

I bet you didn't realize that some of the vendors used on your properties are owned partially by the management company. One time, I hired a management company, only to find out that they owned minor interest in the flooring company, paint company and plumbing company that worked on my properties. Unfortunately, reliability is a huge problem with this method if the jobs weren't properly bid out or were just handed over to vendors who didn't enforce best prices. These dealings are unethical and easily could be considered fraud in a court of law. So, make it clear with your property management company that you have no interest in using vendors that conflict with your existing business.

You are an investor. You are not trying to be a landlord. Therefore, you must live the life of an investor by following the numbers and putting it all online. Look for great deals anywhere and everywhere, not just in your immediate neighborhood. Manage the managers. You probably know how to do this, but I'll share the best techniques I've found over the last 20 years. In eight months, I've made only two visits to a property that cash flows $27,000 per month! Sound great? They are all not like that, but they do exist.

Before hiring any firm, do your homework and check the references of the company you intend to use. Remember, the company or individual that you hire will be managing a very substantial investment of yours, so you must choose wisely. You likely will find a number of property management companies in an online search. A good way to find out which companies are reputable (and which are not) is to ask other investors and property owners for references.

When choosing a property management company, remember that everything is negotiable. The contract you set up with them can be customized to include or exclude a variety of services. I would recommend a 30-day exit clause in case things don't work out. In addition, if you decide to go the route of using a fee management company, you should personally interview the company and representatives who will be working with your investment. Ask questions such as the firm's level of staffing, whether they have in-house maintenance staff and their use (or non-use) of subcontractors. In-house should be cheaper, and therefore create more profit for owners. Using staffing companies should be a red flag, too. Payroll will be too high if the owner has to pay more than just a salary to have employees working at their commercial real estate.

You also should discuss the economics of your contract at this initial meeting, as it is likely that the company will charge a preset percentage of your building's gross revenue. It's a good idea to get a feel up front for how much this amount will be. This fee is typically determined based on the size of the property being managed, as well as the services that will be performed.

A normal fee range for managing a medium-sized building is 2 to 4 percent of the gross rent collected. Although that may seem high, it can be well worth it in various circumstances. Basing the fee on gross revenues also can be a motivating factor for the management company to do a good job; a higher amount of gross or collected rent is an incentive for the management company to collect.

Furthermore, the addition of provisions into the management company contract to exclude late fees and any other ancillary income from the calculation of the management fee will make not just collecting the rent, but collecting it on time, a top priority for the management company.

Be sure that the fee paid to the management company is based on gross revenue rather than net revenue. If the company were to be paid on net income, it would create a potential reverse incentive to not keep up-to-speed on maintenance or other necessary procedures in an effort to boost the bottom line.

Before signing on the dotted line with any property management company, be sure that the fees involved will still fit in with your profit projections on the investment. After all, the whole reason for doing all of this is to make a profit, so be sure that you will still be on track to do so. Even though you are trading your money for the property manager's time, you need to be certain that you are paying for the right amount of time being spent on the right tasks.

Hiring a Professional Property Manager

When you hire a professional property manager, they will be responsible for all management duties related to your property. The primary difference between this type of property management and a fee management company is that the professional property manager will work only for you at your direction.

Depending on the experience and the expertise of the professional property manager, having a full-time individual taking care of your property can, in many ways, be the best of both worlds. In this case, economies of scale can be realized, as can the ability to react quickly to issues as they arise.

The primary duties of the professional property manager will include creating a plan for building improvement, developing a marketing plan, and in some cases, handling financial matters. The property manager should not only be in charge of rent collection. They should have hands-on knowledge of the specific needs of the property—they should essentially be as familiar with the property as you, the owner, are.

As with a fee management company, compensation of a professional property manager is usually tied to the property's performance. In this case, however, a base salary is paid and enhanced by various bonus compensations in return for increased operating performance levels.

Another possible incentive is education and training. Any additional qualifications naturally make the candidates more valuable to you. A professional property manager's qualifications are similar to those of a good, competent fee manager. For example, these individuals may hold a college degree or professional industry designations, such as the CPM, or Certified Property Manager.

Asset Management with Property Managers

Many commercial property management firms can provide strategies to help real estate owners not only manage their properties, but also reduce operating costs and enhance property values. These companies help boost tenant satisfaction by providing tasks related to security, maintenance and management. They will help you keep your property running smoothly and manage the property as the income-producing and appreciating asset that is its purpose.

Budgets and Financial Management of Your Apartment Property

Regardless of who manages your property, keeping track of your property's financial condition is critical to the overall success of your investment. Therefore, your accounting methods need to be up to date.

If you have only a few rental units, you may prefer to keep records in a journal or personal accounting package. Having more than 20 units, however, might require the use of a software package. In any case, the IRS requires that you report your rental property income and expenses on your tax return.

Reducing Expenses

There are many ways to raise your profit margins; one is to reduce your expenses. Often, the difference between positive and negative cash flow is carefully monitored and controlled expenses.

Your highest costs, such as mortgage payments and real estate taxes, are likely fixed, so there is not a lot you can do to reduce them. However, your variable expenses, such as utilities and maintenance costs, can be both managed and controlled. For instance, if heat, air conditioning and hot water are included in your tenants' rental amounts, installing programmed thermostats and timers to control output can help reduce costs.

In apartment buildings, there are cap rates in multiples. Every dollar you save or every dollar you create in a 10-cap market is $10. If you can increase those numbers, you can figure out how to make more money, more cuts and create an extra $100,000 on an apartment building. In a 10-cap market, that's 10 times $100,000. You would have essentially created $1 million out of thin air!

Some additional tips for reducing your expenses include the following:

- Walk through vacant properties after contract vendors have performed services to ensure that the thermostats have been reset to conserve electricity.
- Use low-wattage, energy-efficient light fixtures.
- Use controls on gas-burning fixtures so that they don't heat at the same rate at night as during the day.

- Verify that the correct water and sewage rates are being charged. Also, verify whether those bills are to be taxed or exempted from sales taxes.
- Install cost-effective water flow restrictors.
- Check all mechanical equipment to ensure that each item is running at peak capacity. (For example, boilers and air conditioners should be inspected and adjusted annually.)

Budgeting

You also can reduce expenses simply by preparing an annual budget that ideally includes allocations for repairs and maintenance. You should include the cost of predictable expenses, as well as some funds for emergency or occasional repairs. My property management company provides me with a 12-month budget report.

In addition, your property should be inspected regularly for any areas needing repair. Some repairs may require immediate attention, while others can be budgeted for addressing at a later date.

It might help to obtain information from the property's previous owner, if possible, regarding maintenance costs. You could use these records as a guideline for your own budget preparation. You should request both utility and repair bills, as well as the names of service providers. In addition, you could get estimates from service vendors for possible future repairs.

Remember to budget for annual real estate taxes. You could even establish a designated savings account that is funded monthly by rents to be used for these annual taxes.

Once you have prepared your annual budget, compare the expected rental income against the sum of all budgeted items. Certainly, your expenses should not exceed the expected income.

If, however, your rental income, combined with other financial resources, will not be enough to cover expected expenses, then you will need to reevaluate some of the budgeted items. If you are budgeting for a potential property purchase and you cannot generate the income necessary to exceed your anticipated expenses, this might not be a good property for you to purchase.

CHAPTER 9

TIPS AND STRATEGIES

A critically important question for any investor is, How can I increase my property's value?

You may think that if you have empty units, you will have no income, so it would be easier to leave low-paying tenants in place to avoid having a high vacancy rate with no cash flow. You cannot allow yourself to think this way! Remember: You purchased the property using a set of specific criteria. Upgrades are one of the most common ways to increase value. New flooring, granite countertops—there is no question that you take action that will attract new residents at a higher rent amount.

You should clean a vacant unit as soon as possible after the former tenants leave. This will help prevent pest infestation and odors. The initial cleaning should include the removal of all trash, wiping down appliances and countertops, sweeping and vacuuming the floors, and washing all windows. In addition, the unit might require pest control. Remember, units should not be shown until they are thoroughly cleaned.

Your presentation of a vacant unit should be made with the prospective tenant's lifestyle and preferences in mind. Often, prospective tenants only see walls, floors and ceilings. Therefore, you or your property manager should seek to create an environment that is warm and inviting, and allow the prospect to envision and desire the property as a home.

When showing a unit, avoid letting potential tenants wander around unattended. Always remain nearby and close enough to hear and note any positive or negative comments they might make. In addition, you should be prepared to answer questions about nearby schools, shopping venues, commuting times, local laws and nearby services of interest.

Renting the unit and collecting rent are the keys to successful property management. Maintaining occupancy and reducing down time further increase your income potential. Therefore, you need to do all that you can to keep units occupied as often as possible.

Renewing Leases or Locking the Back Door

Many experts believe that the lease renewal process begins with the move-in orientation. While communicating policies and procedures to residents, you should also focus on developing a good relationship with your tenants and setting a professional and responsive tone for future interactions.

During conversations with new residents, you should clarify whether you, the tenant, or both of you are responsible for the maintenance of common areas. You can offer special instructions for using appliances, such as microwave ovens or washing machines, and you also can explain what to do in case of fire or other emergencies.

Despite your efforts, some residents may choose to move. The national average for small investor resident turnover is 59 percent per year. Residents have many reasons for leaving. They could have an opportunity to rent a unit in another area, or they may be transferred to another location because of their job.

Some ways to develop strong relationships and attempt to reduce turnover by residents include the following:

- Show an interest in their lifestyle and needs during the rental interview.
- Follow through quickly on promises regarding repairs and decorating. Don't offer something that you can't deliver.
- Give residents your phone number, along with other important numbers for emergency repairs or services.
- Respond promptly to service requests. Communication is the key to maintaining good relationships.

- Let residents know in advance what you expect from them and what they can expect from you on such items as rent payment, lease provisions, pets, complaints, services, etc.
- Respect their privacy and right to peaceful possession of their home during their lease period.
- If you must enter a rental unit when the resident is not at home and/or without prior notice, leave a note stating that you were there and why. If possible, however, do not enter a resident's home without giving at least 24-hour notice. Be careful to comply with state laws on this issue.

The less time spent on finding new residents, the more successful you will be. Long-term, stable residents mean an uninterrupted stream of rental income and lower turnover costs, as well as lower maintenance costs since satisfied residents tend to take better care of the property.

To retain solid residents, set up a reward system. Be creative here. For example, help tenants celebrate their anniversary as a resident. When residents have occupied the unit for a year, do something to show your appreciation. Ideas can range from offering discounts on rent to giving them a day's free use of the maintenance staff.

Most rental leases define when a resident must be notified regarding lease expiration, unit inspection and rental increases. In states that do not specify, it is recommended that you begin the renewal process 90 days in advance of the lease expiration.

Depending on state and local laws, residents whose rental units are in unsanitary or damaged condition may not be renewed until a follow-up inspection indicates that the problems have been corrected and/or the resident has paid in full for the corrective work to be completed.

Lease renewal time is a pivotal point in the owner-tenant relationship. This is when residents may request redecorating, carpet cleaning, new appliances or other improvements. During the first year or two, renewals may not warrant improvements. That being said, it is a good policy to repaint the unit and clean the carpet every two or three years. This not only pleases residents, but also keeps up the property's value.

If the property is well maintained and doesn't need redecorating or carpet cleaning, you might give the resident a rent rebate in an amount that is slightly less than what it would cost you for these expenses, or you could consider a small improvement to the property. These gestures on your part also act as an incentive for resident to renew.

A lease is not considered renewed until all of the lease documents are signed and delivered by the appropriate parties. When the renewal process is completed, you should update all resident files and security deposit records.

When obtaining renewals, letters, flyers and other written materials, it is important to convey rental rates quoted and dates of notice delivery in compliance with state laws. However, letters and notices are not substitutes for the personal contact that may be necessary in order to obtain renewals.

Now that you know most of what you need for investing success, I'd like to share my real estate philosophy. You see, for years I was missing something very important: the know-how, systems and processes for financial success. Real estate proved to be a wonderful vehicle to teach me these lessons so that I could pass them on to you, the reader. I didn't understand these processes until I started paying attention to how these factors worked and connected to each other. I learned from books, classes and first-hand experiences in buying houses and finally, apartment buildings. Many of us lose out in business the first time around by not realizing that it takes success in the whole package for this to work, to create something that adds value to the marketplace. We can change neighborhoods one house or apartment building at a time while creating wealth for our investors, ourselves and the entire community.

At first, I didn't have right tools in the toolbox, the software for the computer or the recipe for the cake. But you have this book and lots of other resources to help you connect the dots and succeed in real estate. I spent years trying to shortcut the process and I was getting nowhere fast! Like so many novices, I didn't know any better.

Did you know most people are on a 60-year plan? That's 20 years of school and 40 years of work. That plan certainly held no appeal for me!

I learned the answer through real estate and developed the idea of the cash flow mindset. I learned quickly that the quick fix wasn't just to flip a property for cash. The real value was in the cash flow this process created.

I saw this firsthand one day, when the owner of the building that I both lived and worked in pulled up and I observed him collecting the rent. The owner had something that I never considered up until that moment: the cash flow mind set. What is that? The process is as follows:

1. Set up your cash flow business (office building).
2. Buy what you need with the cash flow.
3. Send out what's left over to work for you.
4. Reinvest what's left over into more cash flow businesses.

I have always considered my dollars to be my warriors in that they better come back to me with more than they left with. In return, I will always respect them, be a responsible steward and, finally, teach their principles to others.

I believe these values are universal among the rich. Living by them removes fear and allows us to follow our joy and experience true freedom and happiness. I achieved this through real estate, and I want my readers to experience this, too.

One commercial real estate deal can change your life forever. It might not be necessary to work and save for 40 years when the end result could be accomplished in months with the use of cash flow from real estate. Instead of slaving away to save $1 million, an alternative might be to figure out why you want the million bucks in the first place. Most of my students say they want a nice house. I always respond, how about $7,000 a month cash flow to pay for that house's mortgage—an obtainable goal in less than a year, and a much better deal than 40 years!

I had to go through these phases and make these connections on my own to really get it. But I did, and so will you! Remember, it's not what you make, but what you do with what you make!

CHAPTER 10

EXIT STRATEGY: POSITIONING PROPERTY TO FLIP OR HOLD, AND CASH FLOW

I have bought and sold thousands of apartment units. I have been through multiple real estate cycles following strategies that I developed firsthand through trial and error. I'm proud to say that I have never lost money in a real estate transaction. I have always done what was right and honorable in my transactions and put my partners' interests before mine. I hope and expect the same for you, too! Be cautious and diligent in your investing.

One of the biggest keys to making money in real estate is to have an exit strategy before you purchase any property. Otherwise, no matter how great your property seems to be, how will you know if, or when, you will ever actually see your return on it? After all, isn't that what investing is all about?

Buying apartment buildings as investments gives you the option to hold and cash flow or flip the property for profit. Knowing how to recognize whether a building is a good value, however, is the most important thing you need to understand before investing in any property.

Therefore, knowing your cap rate is essential. The higher the cap rate, the more risk you will be taking on. With apartment buildings, you have the ability to adjust the cap rate by adjusting the net operating income (NOI). This means that by increasing your rental rates, you can also increase your property rate.

You may need to do some research to determine what the average cap rate is in your area if you want it to be in line with similar property cap rates in the area. In any case, it is important to be educated on how the numbers work and what they mean before making your decision to purchase a property or deciding to hold or flip it.

In our wealth-building strategy, selling the property after nine to 18 months is ideal. However, some parameters must be adhered to if you are going to get top dollar for the property. Otherwise, all of your hard work may not pay off as you had hoped.

The first rule is that the less a buyer has to do to (and for) the property upon taking it over, the more money they will pay. In other words, the less time, hassle and energy that the buyer expects to expend on the property, the more the property will sell for.

For example, if the new buyer has to evict numerous bad tenants and complete costly and time-consuming repairs, they are not likely to offer you anywhere near top dollar for it. However, if the property is in good condition, the tenant mix is good and responsible, the rents are at their highest levels, and the expenses already have been reduced to their lowest level, you likely can expect to sell the property for very close to full price.

Here is where you need to be careful if you want this whole system to work for you. You can purchase the property if it's in a great location and if the building can be filled with great rent-paying tenants. Imagine that right after you purchase the apartment building, you decide that you don't want to do the necessary work to keep the income stream at its highest potential level. You don't want to work on reducing expenses or doing necessary maintenance. In this case, you are not likely to be able to flip the property for anywhere close to what you had hoped.

So, how do you get a property ready to appraise for its highest possible price and accomplish the kind of wealth you have hoped for? Keep the building in top shape, get rid of bad tenants, replace them with good tenants, reduce expenses and bring the property up to date. Next, approach your lender, stating that you would like to refinance the property.

Keep in mind it is the lender—not you—who will decide who the appraiser will be. Make sure the lender uses an appraiser who has experience with apartment buildings. You should also accompany the inspector on the appraisal.

CHAPTER 11

CONTINUING THE WEALTH-BUILDING PROCESS

Once you begin investing in apartment buildings, you will want to be sure you are taking advantage of all available wealth-building aspects. When applied, you will be creating wealth for generations to come.

Revealed Secrets that Pay Off in Real Estate

The following are the four primary areas where you will see your investment pay off.

Appreciation

Appreciation is sometimes referred to as capital gain. Capital gain results from natural inflation, property improvements or both. As long as inflation remains healthy and the economy is growing, a property should be worth more when you sell it than when you bought it.

Equity Buildup

When a property is purchased, equity is defined as the cash investment or down payment. As the mortgage is paid down, the loan principal decreases. This, coupled with the value of the property going up, will give you more equity. This alone is an extremely important wealth-building tool. For some of you it's not easy looking into the future 10 or 20 years. I was like that, but now it's 10 or 20 years later and I still have those properties. And some are almost paid off! That is what I want for you and your families. If you buy right and pay down the debt, these cash flows from the properties will give you the freedom to do what you want—and, most of all, when you want.

Cash Flow

Cash flow is the money netted each month on income-producing properties. Positive cash flow is the leftover money after all rents and income from other related sources have been collected and all expenses have been paid. I call my cash flow my "droid army." I send these dollars out and hope they bring more home. This cash flow process facilitates a lifestyle for you and your family and assists in purchasing more real estate to increase your cash flow.

Tax Shelter Benefits

Tax shelter benefits include depreciation on the property, as well as related benefits. It's my hope that you still have the goal of becoming a millionaire. In doing so, you will step out of your comfort zone and start working with CPA's, bookkeepers and tax advisors. Investors receive many benefits. The government is your partner. They don't want to be in the housing business, so they incentivize others to do it. Tax incentives are important, and you need them to help you through the rough times, too. There are many options, from cost segregation to straight-line deprecation. Ask your CPA what works best for you.

Tax Planning for Additional Wealth Building

Strategic tax planning has become a necessity for real estate owners. Not too long ago, simply buying real estate gave the property owner tax advantages. Annual losses, considered "paper" losses, could be written off against any income. Rental property was considered one of the true tax shelters.

In addition, depreciation terms were shorter. This allowed for a quick write-off of the investment. Even when property was sold, capital gains tax codes allowed the property owner to keep more of the profit.

Today, many items are unable to be expensed. The ability to expense depends on whether the cost is a repair or an improvement. The general rule now is that a repair can be expensed in the current year, while an improvement must be depreciated.

If a cost cannot be expensed in the current year, the next best approach is to depreciate it. You should evaluate the cost and use the shortest permitted period of depreciation. Currently, the depreciable time period for most items found in rental property (such as carpets, refrigerators, appliances and so on) is seven years. The shorter the term used for depreciation, the higher the annual depreciation deduction. By depreciating an item, you can at least portion its cost to offset rental income in the current year.

If an item is unable to be expensed or depreciated, you might be able to amortize it. Any actual cost that cannot be expensed in the current year, depreciated over its life, or amortized over the loan period—but is not specifically disallowed— typically can be added to the basis. Adding to the basis is, however, considered a last resort, because no benefits can be obtained in the current year. The only tax benefit in this particular case occurs when the property is sold.

The 1031 Tax Exchange

You also can avoid capital gains tax altogether if you dispose of one property and exchange it for another. In addition, three-way property exchanges are much easier, due to IRC Section 1031. These changes do not need to be made simultaneously.

If property exchanges are structured properly, in most cases, there will be no income taxes at all due on capital gains. You are able to defer payment of taxes until the properties are sold, or you can even continue to exchange properties and avoid the payment of taxes on capital gains.

In addition, if your heirs are to inherit ownership of your property, they can do so at the property's then-current value as opposed to its old basis or depreciable balance. By exchanging, owners can avoid paying capital gains taxes while they are alive; the same applies to heirs when they acquire the property upon the death of the owner.

Moving Forward

As I mentioned at the beginning of this book, conventional wisdom is NOT ALWAYS CORRECT! This is important to remember. There is a secret that most industry gurus will not share with you, but it is important to stress over and over again because knowing this will speed up your progress.

THE SECRET is that the best deals come up when THEY are ready—not when you are ready. Great deals come in the size and shape that they want—not what you want. They come in the prices and values they choose—not what you choose.

In other words, your ideal deal could be waiting for you tomorrow, or it could be ready six months from now. You always have to be ready, because you simply don't know when it will happen. The most important thing here is to always be ready to go after a good deal when it comes up, and to know with 100 percent certainty that at some point, it will!

That being said, it also is important that you not limit yourself to specific properties or locations. Doing so might mean that really great deals pass you by. You certainly will want to be sure that your properties are in good locations and that you are familiar with the market you are investing in. But do not be so specific that you rule out potentially great deals because they do not fit perfectly into your "ideal deal" mold.

It is important, as you move through your real estate investing career, to get into a position where you have the ability to make larger down payments on your properties. You always want to have enough control to purchase a great property whenever it comes up, because you just never know when the next great deal will appear!

The way to speed up your progress towards wealth in real estate is to be always in a position to jump on a great deal when opportunity knocks. The very best way to do this is by having as much cash available, financing ready and partners geared up to go as you possibly can.

Regardless of what many of the so-called gurus will tell you, this is truly the fastest way to wealth in real estate. By using this in conjunction with the strategies of finding and negotiating great deals, you will win every time.

Always keep in mind the best and fastest path to wealth in real estate is investing in as many great and profitable deals as you possibly can— whenever they come up! The best way to accomplish that is by becoming a cash-generating buyer of projects as quickly as possible. Create a reputation for yourself as a doer and a closer! You will go far and will eventually be sought out.

Now, how much time does somebody need to get involved in this way? A lot of people don't have even a small amount of time to spare. Some have several jobs and child care responsibilities. There are people who are sick and people who are involved in the lending business full-time. How much time will they need to be an investor in real estate?

When I started out, I worked full-time. It was a great, empowering feeling to know that I was creating my escape by buying real estate. It was very exciting and it took little time. I was building my cash flow.

You might like your job and want to continue with it, so it's really up to you. What's your number? Do you need $10,000, $20,000 or $30,000 a month for your dreams? How do we cash flow your dreams? One game-changing apartment deal, like the one I made at the beginning of 2011 (a class C apartment building that generates class A rents), can change your life forever. This one deal pays for my million-dollar home in Houston.

So, if you figure out what you need to do to retire, or how to cover your monthly expenses, then take it one step further and figure out what your dreams cost. I'll figure out with you how many apartment units you'll need to buy.

I remember taking a two-month trip to Japan—eight blissful weeks away from corporate America. When I finally got home, I said, "You know what? I think I've had it." And that was it. I stopped working then and there, because I wanted to. When the time comes, so could you!

A question that people frequently ask is whether my system will work for them. Technically, it's not my system. To add value and rent out a home is one of the oldest business models ever. I have simply tweaked and improved it so that it would work anywhere, and for anyone. It doesn't matter where you are. There are apartment buildings everywhere and there are people making money with them. They are not necessarily people born with silver spoons in their mouths. Many of them have figured out how to invest in apartments. It just takes a little knowledge, and that's what this book is all about.

For some, a great way to get involved in apartment buildings is to invest or join someone else's deal and learn from the experience. Others like diversification in investment classes. I do both: I find my own deals and invest in others. Both experiences have been very profitable for me.

So what will you choose?

You now are equipped with the knowledge and means to literally "fold time" in terms of your returns and growth of your wealth. You have in your hands the necessary steps and strategies to take your real estate investing to the next level. You have the tools to become very wealthy, or to grow your existing wealth into a massive net worth in a very short period of time, versus 40+ years of toil!

Although the methods presented here are not "get rich quick" techniques, they surely will help you create wealth much faster than conventional methods. *Humans, by nature, seek purpose—a cause greater and more enduring than themselves.* One of my mentors had a saying that the more you serve others, the more you will be rewarded. In reality, real estate is simply a means to an end. It can make you wealthier than you are today, and can help you to do so quickly. You must take full advantage of this information and use it to the best of your ability. It's a scalable business that has built in systems and processes that can teach you to excel in many different areas of life.

I wish you all the best in your wealth-building endeavors! Please drop me a line about your successes. I'd love to hear about how I empowered you to be a real estate entrepreneur.

Visit alanschnur.com for free educational videos, tips and strategies!

36182106R00069

Made in the USA
Middletown, DE
26 October 2016